Make Your Own Machine Appliqué

BABY QUILTS

Make Your Own Machine Appliqué

BABY QUILTS

Jane Forward

UNIVERSE BOOKS
New York

All quilts designed and appliquéd by Jane Forward

Book designed by Nancy Carey

Illustrations by Susan Morse Jamback and Robert Jamback. All quilts photographed by Larry McDonald, with the exception of the Toy Shelf quilt, photographed by Robert Hoebermann. Toy Shelf quilt reprinted with permission from McCall's *Needlework & Crafts*.

The patterns in this book are intended for individual home use only. They are not to be used for commercial or manufacturing purposes without written permission from the author.

Published in the United States of America in 1984
by Universe Books
381 Park Avenue South, New York, N.Y. 10016

© 1984 by Jane Forward

84 85 86 87 88 / 10 9 8 7 6 5 4 3 2 1

Printed in the United States of America

Library of Congress Cataloging in Publication Data

Forward, Jane, 1949–
   Baby quilts.

   1. Quilting—Patterns. 2. Children's coverlets.
I. Title.
TT835.F67   1984   746.9'7   84-40353
ISBN 0-87663-445-5
ISBN 0-87663-599-0 (pbk.)

To Rod, Brent, and Janel

CONTENTS

Equipment and Materials, Selecting Fabrics and Colors, Enlarging the
Patterns, Fabric Requirements and Cutting, Backing Fabric, Batting, Quilt
Sizes, Setting Up Your Machine for Zigzag Stitching, Methods of Holding
Appliqués in Place, Starting to Appliqué, Borders, Sewing the Three
Layers Together, Basting, Machine Quilting

INDIVIDUAL QUILT PATTERNS AND INSTRUCTIONS

INTRODUCTION

These baby quilts are pictures. Not simply pictures to look at, but ones to nestle in, sit on, or play peekaboo under. If you can sew, you can soon be wrapping one of these quilts around a baby you love.

The quilts are easy to make because I have designed them for machine appliqué. This technique, unlike the preprinted fabric pictures, is an authentic appliqué and is much easier and faster than handworked appliqué. All you need to master the technique is a sewing machine with a zigzag stitch and some practice. Before starting, read the general information and instructions. Once you are able to produce a consistent stitch on scrap material, you are ready to select a quilt and follow the individual directions for it. While putting forth less effort than earlier generations, you can share their satisfaction in watching a picture emerge as fabric is applied on fabric.

In these quilt designs I have aimed for the simplicity of a child's picture book. This approach to design is quite different from the one used by traditional quilt-makers. Their baby quilts were almost always smaller versions of adult quilts, with emphasis on complex motifs. Why not, I thought, design quilts that would tell a child about the things children have always loved: animals, flowers, toys. I sketched birds, cats, rabbits, and some tulips behind a fence. By enlarging and placing the objects on an uncluttered background, I found I could make them stand out for a child to see. The quilt, a bright comfort for an infant, could later be hung on the wall for a preschooler to enjoy.

But I did not stop with the idea of a wall-hanging. I would dangle a multi-colored balloon mobile above the crib, and let sunshine filter through a rainy-day duck on the window shade. How delighted a child would be to see a frog pond stenciled on the bedroom floor. So I have included a final chapter (for inspiration) on accessories to help you get started. It will give you ideas about how to use the quilt patterns for all kinds of other objects, using other craft techniques as well as sewing.

Since my own two babies are well grown, there is no crib available in my house to display any of my quilts. Instead, I hung watermelon slices above my table and now feast on the thought of summer even with snow nearly up to the windowsills. I think you too will find that some of the quilts can decorate other areas of your home besides the baby's room.

GENERAL INFORMATION
AND INSTRUCTIONS

EQUIPMENT AND MATERIALS

A sewing machine with a zigzag stitch. It should be in good running order, clean, and oiled.

A pair of shears for cutting the largest quilt pieces and a pair of *smaller scissors* for cutting the smaller and more intricate appliqués. They should both be sharp.

Thread. Buy a good-quality cotton-covered polyester thread. Zigzag stitching uses a lot more thread than straight stitching does.

Square for drawing even squares and rectangles.

Sewing machine needles. Size 14 was used on all of the quilts in this book. This size is for medium-weight fabrics. If you are using heavy fabrics, use a size 16; use a size 11 for lightweight fabrics.

Water-soluble fabric marker. Follow the package directions. These markers erase with water.

Fabric glue stick. Follow package directions.

You will also need a yardstick, ruler, pins, hand-sewing needles, seam ripper, tape measure, pencil, ballpoint pen, fine-line black marker, roll of brown wrapping paper, roll (or large sheets) of tracing paper, and dressmaker's carbon paper.

SELECTING FABRICS AND COLORS

Fabrics chosen should be closely woven, washable, and colorfast. Suitable fabrics are cottons, blends, calicos, broadcloths, cotton flannels, ginghams, percales, corduroys, satins, and denims. Unsuitable fabrics are knits, sheers, super-heavy fabrics, rough-textured fabrics, and wools. The last two might irritate a baby's skin. Prewash and dry all fabrics before cutting to eliminate later problems from color running and shrinkage. Look for fabric sales and check out the remnant table. Because a lot of the appliqués require only small amounts of fabric, you may want to use fabric scraps you have on hand.

The colors I have chosen for these quilts are just a guide. Perhaps you want to coordinate the quilt with your own color scheme. Use your imagination when selecting colors (solids and prints). The old rule of pink for girls and blue for boys is still nice, but don't be afraid to use bright colors, too.

A method I sometimes use for selecting colors is to trace or sketch a small version of the quilt on several sheets of paper. Using crayons or markers, I color each one differently, and select the one I like the best.

ENLARGING THE PATTERNS

Most of the patterns are on grids and have to be enlarged. You will need paper a little larger than the full-size pattern. 36″ is the maximum-width paper required for even the largest pattern. Brown wrapping paper sold by the roll is good for enlarging most of the patterns; this comes 30″ wide. If necessary, you can tape two pieces of paper together to get the size you need. Using a yardstick and a ballpoint pen, draw a grid on your paper the size specified on each pattern. With a pencil, draw the lines of the pattern onto the large squares, copying the lines on the smaller squares. Do this square by square. It will help to number the squares across the top and down the right-hand side on both grids. If you don't want to take the time to enlarge the pattern by this method, take the pattern to a printer and have a photostat enlargement made. Draw over the pencil lines of the pattern with a fine-line black marker. Trace each section of the appliqués onto tracing paper. It's important to add a 1/4" seam allowance to the sections of appliqués that are overlapped by another section of appliqué. Use dressmaker's carbon paper to trace the appliqués onto the fabric. Be sure to read the fabric requirements and cutting instructions before cutting out the appliqués. If you are cutting several appliqués the same size (such as the leaves on the Unicorn quilt), make a template by tracing the pattern onto lightweight cardboard; cut it out and draw around it directly onto the fabric. Use the fabric marker for this. Note: The terms *background fabric* and *quilt front* refer to the same section.

FABRIC REQUIREMENTS AND CUTTING

Without cutting diagrams, it is difficult to give exact fabric requirements. You will have an adequate amount of fabric if you use care in laying out and cutting. The fabric requirements given are for 45" wide fabric. Make sure you fit all of the quilt pieces and appliqués onto the fabric for each color before you start to cut. Start with the largest pieces first (quilt fronts and backs). With a yardstick and a fabric marker, draw these lines directly onto the fabric, using a square for the corners. Draw the border strips onto the fabric on the crosswise grain from selvage to selvage. Each strip should abut another. Lay out the appliqués either on the lengthwise or crosswise grain (whichever fits best). Remember to lay out the largest appliqués first and then the smaller ones. Cut out the pieces following in the individual instructions for each quilt.

BACKING FABRIC

Unless you are using a fairly heavy fabric for your quilt front (such as denim), it will be necessary to use two layers of fabric. (The underneath fabric is referred to as the backing fabric from now on.) This will give your quilt front the weight and body needed to prevent puckering when machine appliquéing.

Use a medium-weight cotton or cotton blend for this. Do not use a nonwoven fusible interfacing for the backing as it tends to separate with a lot of handling and creates a drag when machine stitching.

BATTING

The quilt batting is the filling or middle of the quilt. It is sandwiched between the quilt front and the quilt back. It gives the quilt warmth and loftiness. Quilts such as these, with minimal quilting, require a polyester batting. I recommend a medium-weight bonded polyester batting. Do not use cotton batting because, unless you do all-over close-together quilting, the batting will bunch up and shift. Bonded batting will not pull apart with handling, and resists shedding and bunching. It is also washable and fast-drying. You can buy this batting in crib size—45" x 60"—or on a roll in widths of 48", 96", and 108", sold by the yard. The crib-size quilt batting is large enough for all of the quilts except three—the Toy Shelf, Farm Scene, and Unicorn quilts. These will require a larger batting. Note: Use a 1/4" seam allowance for all the straight stitch sewing.

QUILT SIZES

The sizes given for these quilts are approximate and vary from quilt to quilt. You can make them larger by adding more or wider borders. You can make them smaller by leaving off a border or making the borders narrower. If you are enlarging a quilt, be sure to buy enough extra fabric.

SETTING UP YOUR MACHINE FOR ZIGZAG STITCHING

Machine appliquéing is done with a medium-wide close zigzag stitch, often referred to as a satin stitch. It is important to read your sewing machine manual and follow the instructions for zigzag stitching (as each machine is a little different). Here are some general rules to go by. Attach the zigzag presser foot or appliqué presser foot (if your machine has one) and the zigzag throat plate. The zigzag presser foot has a wide needle hole. The appliqué presser foot does too. It also has more open toes and a groove on the bottom for the zigzag stitch to glide through more easily. The zigzag throat plate has a wide needle hole. Thread the machine and bobbin with different color threads. This will help you when you are adjusting tensions. Set the stitch width so that your stitch is just slightly wider than 1/8″. Now set your stitch length so that your stitches are very close together. The smaller the number, the closer together your stitches will be. Your zigzag stitch should be smooth and flat, and appear as a solid line. You should not be able to see the edge of the appliqué through it. However, your stitches should not be so close together that they pile up and cause the machine to bind. Loosen your top thread tension to prevent puckering and your bobbin thread from showing on top. You may also have to reduce the pressure on your presser foot (refer to your manual for this). Once you have your machine properly adjusted, you can sew all of the appliqués with the same color bobbin thread. When changing colors, only the top thread will require changing. Practice stitching on two layers of scrap fabric until you achieve a good satin stitch. Zigzag stitching seems to create even more lint than straight stitching. This will hinder the smooth operation of your machine. Take the time to clean out the lint from the bobbin case and feed dogs often, with a lint brush.

METHODS OF HOLDING APPLIQUÉS IN PLACE

There are four basic methods of holding appliqués in place before machine stitching. The first one is *pinning*: this method is adequate when you are experienced or when the appliqués are simple. Do not stitch over the pins as it may bend or break your sewing machine needle. The second method is with a *fabric glue stick* (it will wash out): this is useful on very small appliqués that cannot be easily basted. Follow the package directions. The third one is *fusible webbing*: this method is good for the more intricate appliqués because it bonds the appliqué completely to the background fabric, but should be used only when necessary because it tends to make the appliqué stiff. I used this method for the cutwork butterfly. To use this method, lay your fabric right side down on an ironing board and lay the fusible webbing on top of this. With the iron set for steam, pass it over the webbing, close without touching it. The hot steam will bond the webbing to the fabric. Cut out the appliqué and bond it into position on the background fabric by steam pressing. The fourth method is *hand basting*: although this method takes more time, it produces satisfying results and I recommend it. With even stitches, baste around the edges of the appliqués. Experiment with each method and see which works best for you.

STARTING TO APPLIQUÉ

If you have never machine appliquéd before, you should start by doing some practice pieces. Cut several different shapes out of scrap fabric. Baste these to two layers of scrap background fabric. The zigzag stitch should cover the edge of the appliqué completely. This prevents loose threads from fraying and makes trimming unnecessary. Start by stitching straight edges of the appliqués. Now stitch some curves. When stitching sharp curves, simply hand-guiding the fabric is not enough. You will have to stop the machine, lift the presser foot, and turn the fabric. When doing this, it is important to leave the needle in the fabric. When stitching an outside curve, leave the needle in the right-hand side of the stitch, turn, and resume stitching. When stitching an inside curve, leave the needle in the left-hand side of the stitch, turn, and resume stitching. You may have to do this several times on a round appliqué. When stitching corners stitch right to the edge, leave the needle in the right-hand side of the stitch, lift the presser foot, turn the corner, and resume stitching. You will stitch over a few of the stitches from the other side. Sharp points are more difficult to stitch. About 1/2" before the point, start turning the fabric toward the point. This will make your stitches a little slanted. When you get to the point, leave the needle in the right-hand side of the stitch, on the very tip of the point. Raise the presser

foot, turn, and resume stitching, turning the fabric to the right until you get 1/2"
beyond the point. Again, you will stitch over a few stitches from the other side.
The stitches will appear mitered. Stitches have a tendency to pile up on these
sharp points. To help prevent this, try stitching more slowly and pulling on the
fabric from the back with your left hand, while guiding the front with your right
hand. *Do not pull too hard.*

Stitching the appliqué's inside details usually requires a narrower zigzag
stitch. All of the details on these quilts were sewn on the machine. Some of
these (such as facial features) require more skill. If you feel this is beyond your
ability, an alternative is hand embroidery. After all the machine appliquéing is
finished, put the quilt front in an embroidery hoop and use three strands of embroidery floss to hand embroider the details with a satin stitch or an outline
stitch. Some of the quilts call for stitching from very narrow to very wide. (An
example is the leaves on the Spring Flowers quilt.) To do this, turn the stitch-
width control as you stitch along without stopping. This will take practice. Turn
the control very slowly. The results should be very even and gradual enlargement of the stitches. If you make a mistake, use the seam ripper to cut the bobbin threads on the back and pull off the top threads.

If you are a beginner at machine appliquéing, I suggest you start by making
the Balloon, the Pastel Geometric, or the Watermelon Pinwheel quilt. These
quilts are the simplest and are easier to appliqué than the others.

BORDERS

Borders add the finishing touch to a quilt and give it a framed effect. Pin a
border strip (right sides together) to each side of the quilt. Sew using a 1/4"
seam allowance. Trim the ends so that they are even with the top and bottom,
and press the seams flat. Now pin a border strip across the top and bottom, including the side borders. Sew, trim the ends, and press again. Repeat this pro-
cedure for second and third borders.

SEWING THE THREE LAYERS TOGETHER

Sew the quilt front to the quilt back and batt as follows. On a large flat surface, lay out the quilt back right side up. Center the quilt front on top of this, right sides together. Smooth out with your hands and pin around the edges. Sew around the edges using a 1/4″ seam allowance, and leave a 12″ opening for turning on one of the sides. Trim the back to match the front edge. Lay out the quilt batt and center the quilt back and front on top of this. Smooth out and pin around the edges. Sew over the first stitching leaving the same 12″ opening. Trim off the excess batt and clip the corners. Turn the quilt right side out. Turn in the edges of the opening and hand sew them together.

BASTING

Basting is necessary to temporarily hold the three layers (front, batting, and back) of the quilt in place before machine quilting. It's important to take the time to do a good job of basting. Your machine quilting will be only as good as your basting. Lay out the quilt on a large flat surface. Using nice even stitches, hand baste down the center from top to bottom. Next, baste rows out to each side about every 6″. Smooth the quilt out with your hands as you baste. Now baste across the middle from side to side. Baste rows toward the top and bottom about every 6″.

MACHINE QUILTING

Machine quilting is sewing through all three layers of the quilt with a straight stitch. This prevents the batting from shifting. These quilts are "outline quilted," that is, stitched around the outside edges of the appliqués. The edges of the borders are also quilted. This makes the appliqués stand out and gives dimension to the quilt. Baby quilts are especially suitable for machine quilting because of their small size. They are much easier to maneuver on a sewing machine than a full size quilt would be.

Again, refer to your sewing machine manual to set your machine for quilting. Attach your presser foot and throat plate for straight stitching. Use the same size needle that you appliquéd with. Set your stitch length to 8 stitches per inch and reduce the pressure on your presser foot. Thread the top of your machine with thread to match the background color of the quilt front. Thread the bottom with thread to match the quilt back. Practice quilting stitches on scraps of fabric with a piece of batting in the middle. Adjust your tension so you cannot see the bobbin thread on the top of your stitch and vice versa. Start quilting by sewing around the edges of the most central appliqués first; then sew out toward the edges. Stitch very close to the edge of the appliqués on the background fabric. Stitch the edges of the borders last. Roll up the excess part of the quilt to fit under the sewing machine arm.

PATTERNS

BUNNIES

Five little tan bunnies framed in their white and green circles.

Finished size is 39" x 49"

FABRIC REQUIREMENTS:

2 3/4 yards light green print
7/8 yard pink print
1/2 yard white
1/4 yard tan
a scrap of light pink
1 yard backing fabric
44" x 54" quilt batt
Thread: white, pink, brown, and green

CUTTING INSTRUCTIONS:

From the light green print, cut individual strips which, when sewn together, will form one border 3 1/2" wide by 5 yards long. Cut the back 44" x 54". Also cut 5 large circles and 4 dividers. From the pink print, cut the front 31" x 41". From the white, cut 5 small circles. From the tan, cut 5 bunnies. Cut the ear centers and noses from the scrap of pink. Cut the backing fabric the same size as the front and baste to the wrong side. Trace the stitching lines onto the bunnies with the dressmaker's carbon paper.

SEWING INSTRUCTIONS:

Using the photo as a guide, position the appliqués onto the front and baste. Machine zigzag around the edges of the appliqués first and then do the details as follows. Use white thread on the circles and dividers. Use brown thread for all parts of the bunnies except for the ear centers and noses; use matching thread on these. Use a narrower stitch for the whiskers and to outline the eye. Stitch the eye centers with a wider stitch. Clip all threads and remove the bastings from the appliqués.

Sew the border strips together and press seams. Now sew on the white borders, doing the sides first and then the top and bottom. Remember to press seams after sewing on each border section. Next, sew on the green print borders in the same order. Press the whole quilt front. Sew the quilt front to the quilt back and batt by referring to the general instructions. Baste all three layers together. Machine quilt around both circles, around the dividers, and on both edges of the white border. Remove bastings.

DUCK

The little duck will stay dry in the rain with his umbrella and rubber boots.

Finished size is 38 1/2'' x 48''

FABRIC REQUIREMENTS:

2 3/8 yards blue and green plaid
1/2 yard white
1 yard medium green
1/4 yard yellow
a scrap of orange and black
1 yard backing fabric
43 1/2'' x 53'' quilt batt
Thread: white, navy, orange, black,
    and yellow

CUTTING INSTRUCTIONS:

From the blue and green plaid, cut individual strips which, when sewn together, will form one border 2 3/4'' wide by 5 1/8 yards long. Cut the back 43 1/2'' x 53'' and cut the top section of the umbrella. From the white, cut the duck. From the green, cut the front 34 1/2'' x 43 1/2''. From the yellow, cut the umbrella's bottom section and handle, and cut the boots. Cut the duck's bill from the orange and his eye from the black. Cut the backing fabric the same size as the front and baste to the wrong side. Trace all the stitching lines onto the appliqués with the dressmaker's carbon paper.

SEWING INSTRUCTIONS:

Using the photo as a guide, position the appliqués onto the quilt front and baste. Machine zigzag around the edges of the appliqués first and then do the details as follows. Cut a slit on the stitching line in the tops of the boots and insert the bottoms of the legs. Use navy thread on the yellow appliqués. Use yellow thread on the three inside top umbrella lines. Use matching thread on the rest. Stitch in the boot buttons with a wider stitch, and use a narrower stitch for the loops. Clip all threads and remove bastings from the appliqués.

Sew the border strips together and press seams. Sew on the plaid borders, doing the sides first and then the top and bottom. Press seams after sewing on each section. Sew the quilt front to the quilt back and batt by referring to the general instructions. Baste all three layers together. Machine quilt around the duck and the umbrella, and on the inside edge of the plaid border. Remove bastings.

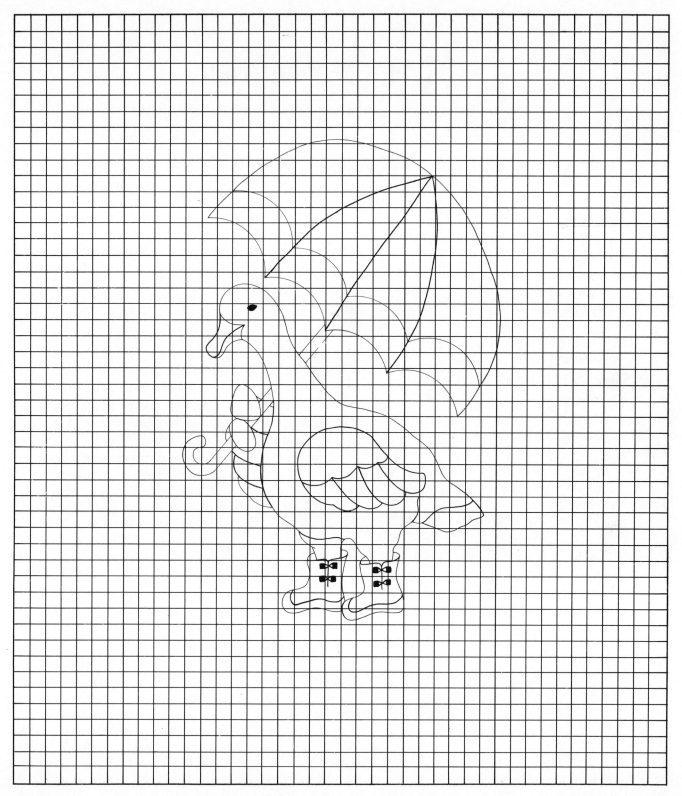

1 square = 1''

PASTEL GEOMETRIC

This pastel geometric quilt is as soft and subtle as a watercolor painting.

Finished size is 36" x 46 1/2"

FABRIC REQUIREMENTS:

2 3/8 yards lavender
5/8 yard white
5/8 yard light aqua
1/8 yard yellow
1/8 yard peach
5/8 yard backing fabric
41" x 51 1/2" quilt batt
Thread: white and lavender

CUTTING INSTRUCTIONS:

From the lavender, cut border strips 2 3/4" wide by 1 1/2 yards long, also border strips 3 3/4" wide by 6 yards long. Cut the back 41" x 51 1/2", and cut 12 half ovals. From the white, cut six 10 1/2" squares for the fronts. From the light aqua, cut border strips 3 3/4" wide by 4 yards long and cut 12 half ovals. From the yellow, cut 12 half ovals. From the peach, cut 12 half ovals.

SEWING INSTRUCTIONS:

From the backing fabric, cut 6 squares the same size as the fronts and baste to the wrong side.

Using the photo as a guide, arrange appliqués onto the front squares overlapping one another and baste. Machine zigzag around the edges using white thread on all of them. Clip all threads and remove bastings.

Sew the border strips together and press seams. Join the two top squares together by sewing on a wider lavender border between them. Do the same for the middle and bottom squares. Press all seams. Now join the top section to the middle by sewing on a narrower lavender border. Do the same for the middle and bottom sections. Next, sew on the light aqua and lavender borders doing the sides first and then the tops and bottoms. Remember to press after sewing on each border.

Sew the quilt front to the quilt back and batt by referring to the general instructions. Baste all three layers together. Machine quilt around each design, on both edges of the lavender borders and on both edges of the light aqua borders. Remove bastings.

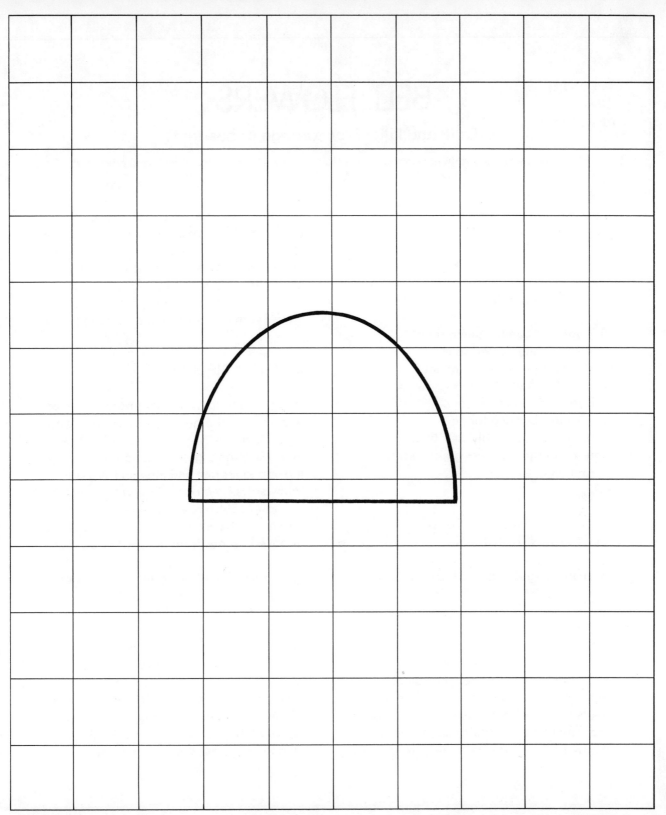

1 square = 1"

BELL FLOWERS

(Quilt and Pillow for carriage or bassinet)

Set against a shiny satin background, pink flowers make for an elegant quilt and pillow set.

Finished quilt is 25″ x 33″
Finished pillow is 11″ x 15″

FABRIC REQUIREMENTS:

3/4 yard burgundy quilted satin
3/4 yard white quilted satin
1 1/8 yards white cotton flannel
1/8 yard pink velour
1/8 yard dark green velour
1 1/8 yards backing fabric
One 12 oz. bag of polyester fiberfill
Thread: burgundy, dark green, white,
   and pink

CUTTING INSTRUCTIONS:

From the burgundy quilted satin, cut the quilt front 25 1/2″ x 33 1/2″. From the white quilted satin, cut the large ovalish appliqué and cut the pillow front 11 1/2″ x 15 1/2″. From the white cotton flannel, cut the quilt back 28″ x 36″ and cut the pillow back 11 1/2″ x 15 1/2″. From the pink velour, cut 15 bell flowers. From the dark green velour, cut 5 sets of leaves and 15 calyxes. Cut the backing fabric the same size as the quilt and pillow front, and baste to the wrong sides.

To round off the edges of the quilt and pillow, fold the fronts in half twice so that the four corners are together. Using a compass, draw a rounded edge on the top corner. Cut on this line through all four layers so they are even. Trace the stitching lines onto the leaves with the dressmaker's carbon paper.

SEWING INSTRUCTIONS:

Using the photo as a guide, position the appliqués onto the quilt and pillow fronts and baste. Draw in the stems with a light pencil line. Machine zigzag around the edges of the appliqués first and then do the details as follows. Use matching thread for all of the appliqués. Stitch over the pencil lines in dark green for the stems. Clip all threads and remove bastings from the appliqués.

Lay out the quilt back right side up. Center the quilt front on this with the right side down. Stitch around the edge of the quilt front using a 1/4″ seam allowance and leaving a 10″ opening for turning. Trim the back to the edge of the front and clip the corners. Turn the quilt right-side-out and hand sew the opening closed. Do the same for the pillow leaving a smaller opening for turning. Stuff the pillow with the polyester fiberfill and hand sew the opening closed.

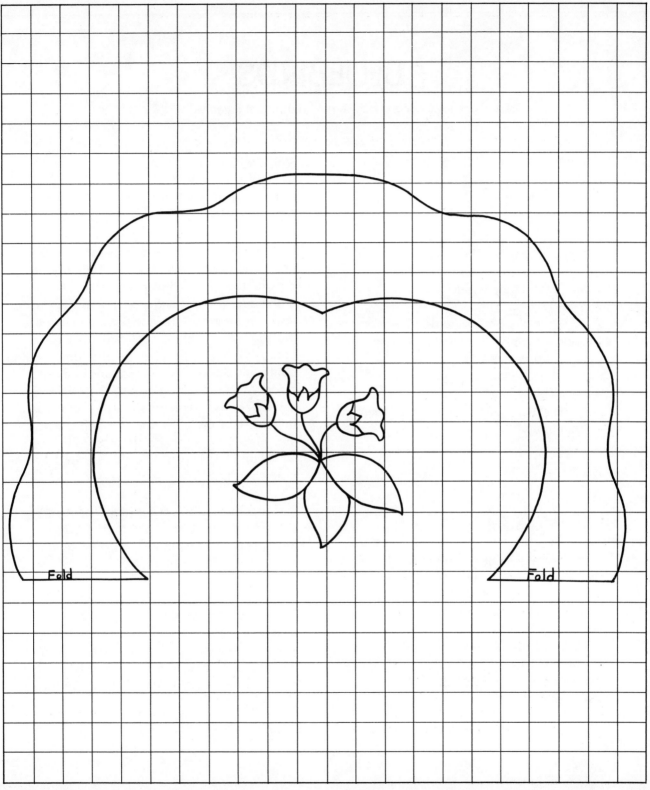

Fold

Fold

1 square = 1″

BLUEBIRDS

Mother and baby bluebirds fly close together.

Finished size is 40 1/2" x 50 1/2"

FABRIC REQUIREMENTS:

2 3/4 yards medium blue
7/8 yard white
7 1/2 yards of 2 3/4" wide floral trim or
    approximately 1 yard of lengthwise
    floral stripe fabric
1 yard backing fabric
45" x 55" quilt batt
Thread: white, and a blue a little darker
    than the fabric

CUTTING INSTRUCTIONS:

From the medium blue, cut the diamond border strips 4 1/2" wide by 2 3/8 yards long. Cut the edge border strips 3 1/4" wide by 5 1/4 yards long. Cut the back 45" x 55". Also cut 3 small and 3 large birds facing left. Cut 2 small and 2 large birds facing right. Trace the stitching lines onto the birds with the dressmaker's carbon paper. From the white, cut the front 31" x 41".

SEWING INSTRUCTIONS:

Cut the backing fabric the same size as the front and baste to the wrong side. Mark the center of all four sides of the front. Sew the border strips together and press seams. With the floral border strips, lay out a diamond so that the four points match the centers of the quilt sides. With the wider blue border strips, make a diamond inside the floral one so that the edges are touching each other. Using the photo as a guide, position the birds onto the quilt front. Baste the diamonds and birds into place. Machine zigzag around the edges of the appliqués first and then do the details as follows. Use the blue thread on all except the outside edge of the floral border; use white on this. Clip all the threads and remove bastings from the appliqués.

Sew on the floral border strips doing the sides first and then the top and bottom. Remember to press the seams after sewing on each border section. Now sew on the blue border in the same order. Press the whole quilt front. Sew the quilt front to the quilt back and batt by referring to the general instructions. Baste all three layers together. Machine quilt around the birds, on the edges of the diamonds, and on both edges of the outside floral border. Remove bastings.

1 square = 1"

DALMATIAN

The little Dalmatian is all set to race his red wagon to the fire.

Finished size is 39" x 49"

FABRIC REQUIREMENTS:

3 yards navy print
1/2 yard red
1/2 yard green
1/4 yard white
a scrap of black
7/8 yard backing fabric
44" x 54" quilt batt
Thread: black, navy, and green

CUTTING INSTRUCTIONS:

From the navy print, cut border strips 2 1/2" wide by 5 3/8 yards long. Cut the front 28" x 38 1/2" and the back 44" x 54". Also cut the small centers of the wheels. From the red, cut border strips 2" wide by 4 3/4 yards long. Cut the hat, wagon, and wheel hubcaps. From the green, cut border strips 2" wide by 4 1/2 yards long. Also cut the wheels and the wagon handle. From the white, cut the dog. From the black, cut the dog's spots, nose, and eye.

SEWING INSTRUCTIONS:

Cut the backing fabric the same size as the front and baste to the wrong side. Trace all stitching lines on the appliqués with the dressmaker's carbon paper. Using the photo as a guide, position the appliqués onto the quilt front and baste. Machine zigzag around the edges of the appliqués first and then do the details as follows. Use navy thread on the hat, wagon, hubcaps, and centers. Use black thread on the dog, spots, nose, and eye. Use green thread on the wheels and wagon handle. To make the tiny spots on the dog's snout, use a narrower stitch and just sew a few stitches for each spot. Clip all threads and remove bastings from the appliqués.

Sew the border strips together and press seams. Sew on the borders in the order of green, red, and navy print, doing the sides first and then the top and bottom. Remember to press seams after sewing on each border section. Now sew the quilt front to the quilt back and batt by referring to the general instructions. Baste all three layers together. Machine quilt around the dog, wagon, on both edges of the green border, and on the outside edge of the red border. Remove bastings.

1 square = 1"

TOY SHELF

Shelves full of toys to catch baby's attention.

Finished size is 45" x 54"

FABRIC REQUIREMENTS:

4 3/8 yards blue with white dots
2 yards white
1/4 yard green print
1/8 yard navy print
1/8 yard orange
1/4 yard light blue print
a scrap of red, blue, flesh,
    green, yellow, pink, navy,
    and green-on-white print
1 yard backing fabric
50" x 59" quilt batt
Thread: blue, medium green, red, white,
    navy, yellow, orange, pink
11 yards 1" wide navy bias tape

CUTTING INSTRUCTIONS:

From the blue with white dots, cut individual strips which, when sewn together, will form one border 7" wide by 5 1/8 yards long, and cut two pieces 25" x 59" each for the back and sew together. Also cut the teddy bear, train, tops and sides of the blocks, and the box of the jack-in-the-box. From the white, cut the quilt front 31 1/2" x 40 1/2". From the green print, cut the guitar's top and knob, ball, doll's dress and booties, car, and the base of the stacking toy. From the navy print, cut the teddy bear's paws, inner ears, and feet, the stripes on the ball, the wheels, top, and front of the train, the arms and hat of the jack-in-the-box, and the tires of the car. From the light blue, cut the teddy bear's snout, the train window, and small front oval, the fronts of the blocks and the body, and front section of the jack-in-the-box. From the orange, cut the teddy bear's bow, the ball's stars, the train's whistles and fender, the doll's hair, the jack-in-the-box's hair, and the fourth ring of the stacking toy.

From the green-on-white print, cut the center of the guitar, the doll's bodice and bow, and the car's windows, hubcaps, and fenders. From the green, cut the guitar's sides and top, and the third ring of the stacking toy.

From the flesh, cut the doll's face, arms, and legs, also cut the jack-in-the-box's face and

(continued)

1 square = 1"

TOY SHELF

(continued)

hands. From the red, blue, and yellow, cut the remaining sections of the stacking toy. Also cut a red nose for the jack-in-the-box. From the pink, cut the mouths for the doll and the jack-in-the-box. From the navy, cut the eyes for the doll, the jack-in-the-box and teddy bear, also teddy's nose.

SEWING INSTRUCTIONS:

Cut the backing fabric the same size as the front and baste to the wrong side. Trace all stitching lines onto the appliqués with dressmaker's carbon paper. Draw a light pencil line across the quilt front 12 1/2" from the top, a second one 25 1/2" from the top, and a third 39" from the top. Sew the navy bias tape across these lines placing the top edge of the tape on the pencil line. Using the photo as a guide, position the appliqués onto the quilt front and baste. Machine zigzag around the edges first and then do the details as follows. Use navy thread on all sections of the teddy bear, stitch in the eyebrows and mouth with a narrower stitch. Use matching thread on all sections of the ball. For the train use navy thread on the light blue print and blue dot sections, white thread on the wheel spokes, and matching thread on the rest. Use green thread for all sections of the guitar except the bar across the bottom, the strings and dots (use white for these). Use a straight stitch for the strings. Trace on the lines for the crank and stitch on the knob in green. For the blocks, use navy thread and stitch in the letters with a wider orange stitch. Use green thread on the doll's dress, booties and bow, and matching thread for the rest. Stitch in doll's eyelashes, nose, and eyebrows using a narrower stitch and navy thread. For the jack-in-the-box use navy thread on the box, body, arms, hat, eyes, and eyebrows. Use matching thread on the rest. For the car use green thread on all sections except the tires; use navy thread on these. For the stacking toy use matching thread on all sections. Clip all threads and remove the bastings from the appliqués.

Sew the border strips together and press seams. Sew on the blue dot border sides first then the top and bottom. Be sure to press after sewing on each border section. Lay out the quilt back right side down, place the quilt batt on top of the back. Now center the quilt front on top of this right side up. Baste all three layers together. Trace the scalloped pattern around the blue dot border 1/4" from the edge. Use a straight stitch to stitch around this line through all three layers. Trim around 1/4" from the stitching line. Open up one edge of the bias tape, place the fold line on the stitching line right sides together, and stitch around the scallops. Stop and pivot the needle between each scallop. Now turn the edge of the bias tape to the back and hand stitch around. You will have to take a tuck between each scallop. Machine quilt around each appliqué, along the bottom of each shelf, and on the inside edge of the blue border. Remove bastings.

SPRING FLOWERS

Spring is in the air with these colorful tulips and daffodils behind the white fence.

Finished size is 38 1/2" x 52 1/2"

FABRIC REQUIREMENTS:

3 yards black print
7/8 yard white
3/8 yard green
1/8 yard rose
1/8 yard yellow
3/4 yard backing fabric
43 1/2" x 57 1/2" quilt batt
Thread: white, black, and green

CUTTING INSTRUCTIONS:

From the black print, cut the front 27"x 41 1/2", the back 43 1/2" x 57 1/2" and border strips 3 1/2" wide x 5 1/4 yards long. From the white, cut 16 fence sections and border strips 1 3/4" wide x 4 7/8 yards long. From the green, cut border strips 2 1/4" wide x 4 1/2 yards long. From the yellow, cut 12 daffodils. From the pink, cut 6 tulips. Trace all stitching lines onto the appliqués with dressmaker's carbon paper.

SEWING INSTRUCTIONS:

Cut the backing fabric the same size as the front and baste to the wrong side. Using the photo as a guide, position appliqués onto the front and baste. Place each fence section so they touch each other and line up the bottoms with the bottom edge of the front. Machine zigzag stitch around the edges of each appliqué first and then stitch in the details as follows. Use white thread on all the appliqués. Use green thread to make the leaves, and starting at the top, put the stitch width control knob on very narrow and gradually turn it to the widest as you sew along. Stitch a stem for each flower, clip all threads, and remove the bastings from the appliqués.

Sew the border strips together and press seams. Sew the borders to the front in the order of green, white, and black print. Always sew on the side borders first, press, and then sew on the top and bottom borders. Now sew the quilt front to the quilt back and batt by referring to the general instructions. Baste the three layers together. Starting at the center of the quilt, machine quilt from top to bottom. Continue to quilt out to the sides every 3 1/4". This should come between each fence section. Do not quilt over the flowers or fence sections, just stop when you come to a flower and start again at the end of it. Quilt along both edges of the green border and along the inside edge of the black print border. Remove bastings.

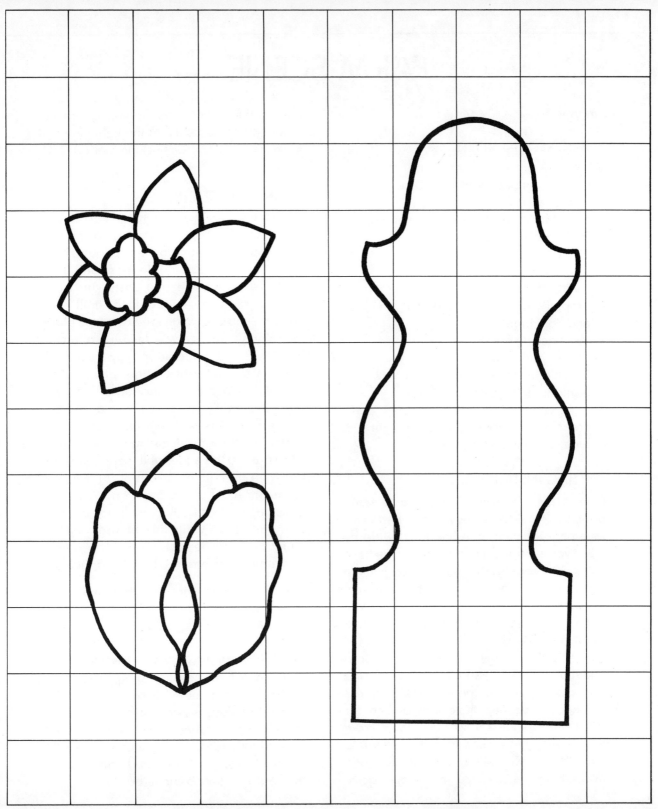

FARM SCENE

Finished size is 44" x 54"

FABRIC REQUIREMENTS:

4 1/4 yards green and white print
5/8 yard light blue print
1/4 yard red print
1/4 yard a different green and white print
  (barn roof)
1/4 yard dark green print
1/4 yard white
1/4 yard brown
a scrap of yellow, black, medium green,
  and light blue
1 yard backing fabric
49" x 59" quilt batt
1/2" wide bias tape, 1 yard each of red,
  orange, pink, green, and blue
Thread: white, black, medium green, dark
  green, red, orange, pink, blue, light
  blue, yellow, and brown

CUTTING INSTRUCTIONS:

From the 4 1/4 yards of green and white
print, cut individual strips which, when sewn
together, will form one border 4" wide by
5 3/4 yards long. Cut two pieces for the back
25" x 59" and sew together. Also cut the
grass section. From the light blue print, cut
the sky section. Leave enough on the bottom
edge to underlap the grass. From the red
print, cut the barn and the silo. From the 1/4
yard of green and white print, cut the barn
and silo roofs, doors, and windows. From the
dark green print, cut the tree top. From the
white, cut two sheep, the clouds, and border
strips 1 1/2" wide x 5 1/4 yards long. From
the brown, cut the road and the tree trunk.
From the yellow, cut the sun and three little
ducks. From the black, cut the sheeps' faces,
ears, and legs. From the medium green, cut
three little lily pads. From the light blue, cut
the duck pond. Cut the backing fabric 35 1/2"
x 45".

SEWING INSTRUCTIONS:

Place the sky and grass on top of the backing
fabric and overlap the grass onto the sky.
Trace stitching lines onto the appliqués. Now
using the photo as a guide, position all the
appliqués into place and baste. Trace the
fence and rainbow lines onto the quilt front.
Baste the top edge of the red bias tape along
the rainbow line. Now continue basting the
bias tapes under the red so they touch each
other in the order of orange, pink, green,
and blue. Place the lower edges under the
grass section. Stitch very close to each edge
of the bias tape with a straight stitch and
matching threads. Now machine zigzag
stitch around the edges of the appliqués first
and then stitch in the details as follows. Use
white thread for the barn and roof and
matching threads for the rest. Stitch over the
fence lines with white thread, use a slightly
wider stitch for the posts. Clip all the threads
and remove the bastings from the appliqués.

Sew the border strips together and press.
Now sew a white border strip to each side of
the quilt front, press, and sew on the top and
bottom borders. Do the same for the green
and white print borders. Press the whole
quilt front. Now sew the quilt front to the
quilt back and batt by referring to the
general instructions on finishing. Baste the
three layers together. Machine quilt around
all the appliqués, along each edge of the
rainbow, sky, grass line, and each edge of
the white border. Remove bastings.

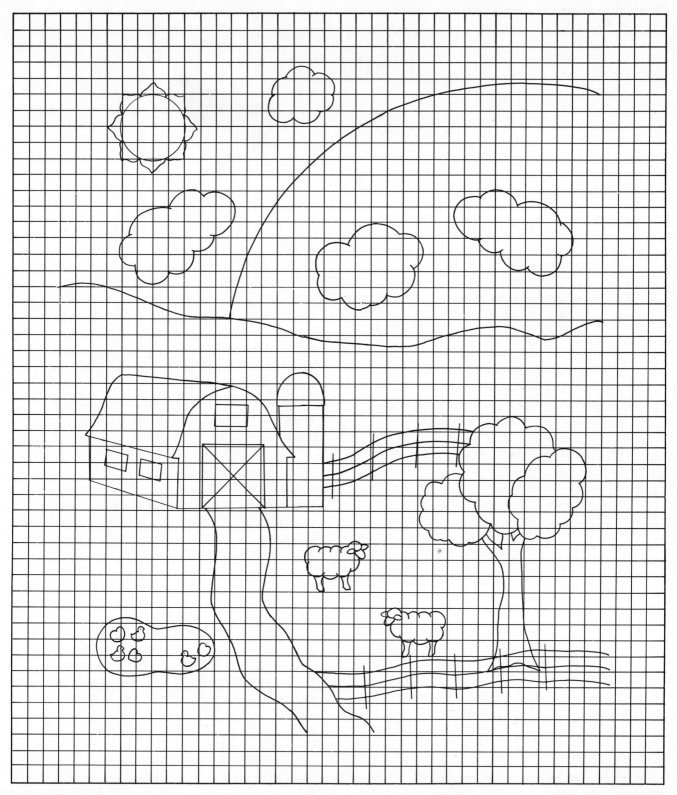

1 square = 1"

UNICORN

The sleepy little unicorn is taking a nap under the peach tree.

Finished size is 43 1/2" x 53"

FABRIC REQUIREMENTS:

3 5/8 yards medium green print
1 yard light blue
1/4 yard peach print
1/4 yard light green
1/4 yard dark green print
1/8 yard peach velour
1/8 yard dark green velour
1/2 yard white
1 yard backing fabric
49" x 58" quilt batt
Thread: peach, light green, dark green,
   medium green, and light blue

CUTTING INSTRUCTIONS:

From the medium green print, cut individual strips which, when sewn together, will form one border 5 1/2" wide by 5 3/8 yards long. Cut the two pieces for the back 29 1/4" x 49" each and sew together. Also cut the grass section. From the light blue, cut the front 34" x 44". From the peach print, cut the third mountain behind the unicorn. From the light green, cut the second and fourth mountain sections behind the unicorn. From the dark green print, cut the first mountain behind the unicorn. From the peach velour, cut 10 peaches. From the dark green velour, cut 36 leaves. From the white, cut the unicorn.

SEWING INSTRUCTIONS:

Cut the backing fabric the same size as the front and baste to the wrong side. Trace all stitching lines onto the appliqués with dressmaker's carbon paper. Using the photo as a guide, position the appliqués onto the front and baste. Machine zigzag around the edges of the appliqués first and then do the details as follows. Use light green thread on the unicorn and matching thread on the rest. Referring to the photo, draw a light pencil line for the branches and stems of the leaves. Now stitch over these in a slightly wider stitch using dark green thread. Clip all threads and remove all bastings from the appliqués.

Sew the border strips together and press seams. Sew on the borders (sides first and then top and bottom). Remember to press after sewing on each border section. Sew the quilt front to the quilt back and batt by referring to the general instructions. Baste all three layers together. Machine quilt around the unicorn, along each mountain top, and on the inside edge of the border. Also machine quilt three vertical lines on the sky section. Do the first one in the center and then measure 8 1/2" out from the center on each side. Do not stitch over the leaves or peaches. Remove bastings.

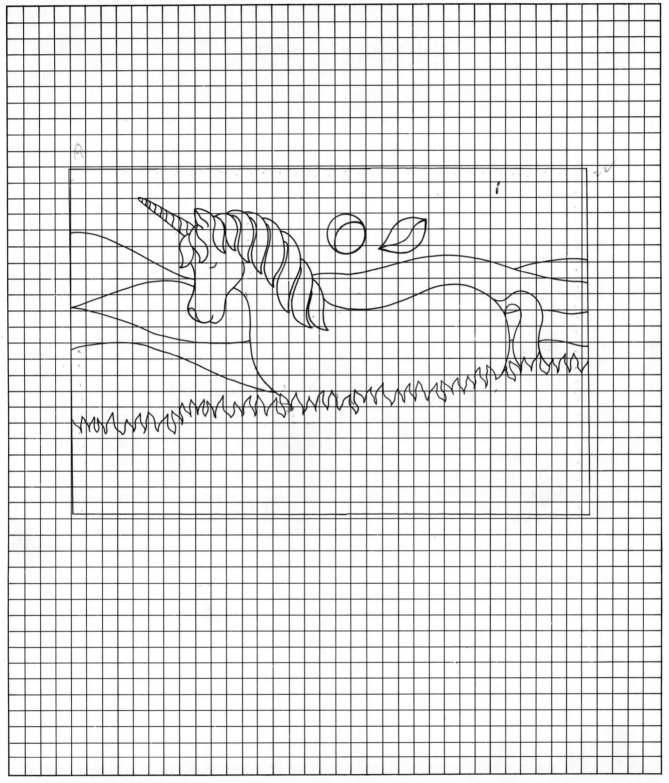

1 square = 1"

SUNFLOWERS

The ladybugs are sunning themselves on the sunflowers.

Finished size is 34" x 44"

FABRIC REQUIREMENTS:

2 yards dark green
7/8 yard white
5/8 yard yellow
a scrap of red and black
7/8 yard backing fabric
39" x 49" quilt batt
Thread: dark green, yellow, red, black,
   and tan

CUTTING INSTRUCTIONS:

From the dark green, cut border strips 2 3/4" wide by 4 5/8 yards long, the back 39" x 49", and two leaf sections of the sunflowers. From the white, cut the front 27 1/2" x 37 1/2". From the yellow, cut border strips 2" wide by 4 1/4 yards long and cut two sunflowers. From the black, cut two ladybugs. From the red, cut two wing sections for the ladybugs. Trace all stitching lines onto the appliqués with the dressmaker's carbon paper.

SEWING INSTRUCTIONS:

Cut the backing fabric the same size as the front and baste to the wrong side. Using the photo as a guide, position the appliqués onto the front and baste. Machine zigzag around the edges of the appliqués first and then do the details as follows. Use tan thread for the center circle of each sunflower and matching thread for the rest. For the spots on the ladybug's wings use black thread and sew just a few short stitches and reverse. Clip all threads and remove bastings from the appliqués.

Sew the border strips together and press seams. Next, sew on the yellow borders, sides first, and then the top and bottom. Be sure to press seams after sewing on each border section. Now sew on the dark green borders in the same order. Press the whole quilt front. Sew the quilt front to the quilt back and batt by referring to the general instructions. Baste the three layers together. Machine quilt around each sunflower, the outside edge of the tan circle, the ladybugs, and on each edge of the yellow border. Remove bastings.

1 square = 1"

SLEEPY CATS

Sleepy cats snooze on their plump pillows.

Finished size is 34 1/2″ x 47 1/2″

FABRIC REQUIREMENTS:

1 7/8 yards brown
7/8 yard brown print
5/8 yard tan
3/4 yard mauve
7/8 yard backing fabric
39 1/2″ x 52 1/2″ quilt batt
Thread: brown, mauve, and tan

CUTTING INSTRUCTIONS:

From the brown, cut border strips 2 3/4″ wide by 4 7/8 yards long and cut the back 39 1/2″ x 52 1/2″. From the brown print, cut two rectangles 19 3/4″ x 27 1/2″ for the fronts. From the tan, cut border strips 2″ wide by 5 1/4 yards long and cut two cats. From the mauve, cut two pillows.

SEWING INSTRUCTIONS:

Trace all stitching lines onto the appliqués with the dressmaker's carbon paper. From the backing fabric, cut two rectangles the same size as the fronts and baste to the wrong side. Using the photo as a guide, position the appliqués onto the fronts and baste. Machine zigzag stitch around the edges of the appliqués first and then do the details as follows. Use brown thread on the cats and matching thread on the pillows. Clip all threads and remove the bastings from the appliqués.

Sew the border strips together and press seams. Join the top and bottom cats by sewing on a tan border across the middle. Now sew a tan border to each side, and then across the top and bottom. Be sure to press seams after sewing on each border section. Next, sew the brown borders on sides first and then top and bottom. Press the whole quilt front. Sew the quilt front to the quilt back and batt by referring to the general instructions. Baste the three layers together. Machine quilt around each cat and pillow and on both edges of the tan borders. Remove bastings.

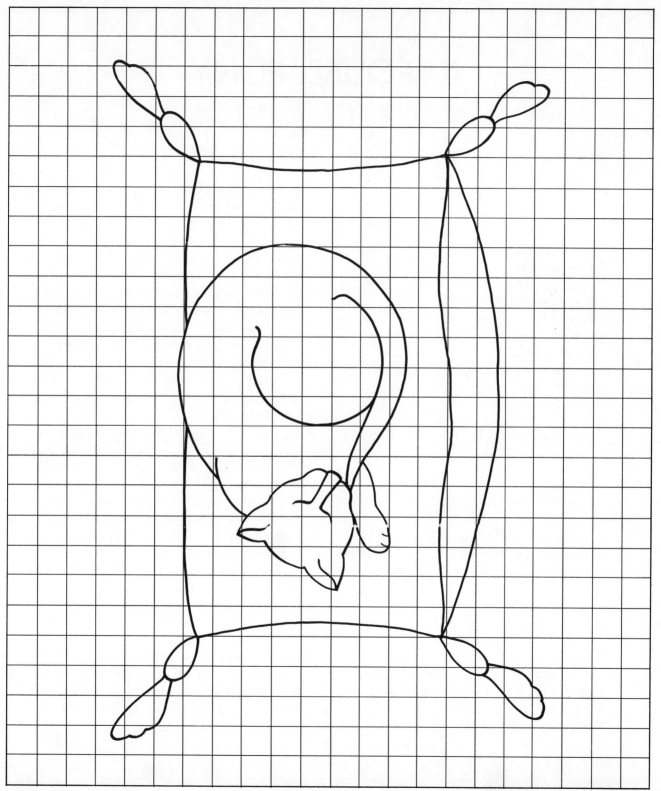

1 square = 1"

CAROUSEL PONY

A prancing carousel pony to decorate baby's room.

Finished size is 36" x 46"

FABRIC REQUIREMENTS:

2 7/8 yards mauve print
3/4 yard light gray
1/2 yard white
1/8 yard maroon
1/8 yard navy
1/4 yard navy print
a scrap of black
3/8 yard black double fold bias tape
1 yard backing fabric
41" x 51" quilt batt
Thread: white, gray, mauve, navy,
    and black

CUTTING INSTRUCTIONS:

From the mauve print, cut border strips 3 1/4" wide by 2 1/4 yards long and border strips 1 3/4" wide by 5 yards long. Also cut the front 33" x 37 1/2" and the back 41" x 51". From the light gray, cut the pony. From the white, cut border strips 1 1/2" wide by 4 1/2 yards long. Also cut the pony's tail, mane, and top saddle blanket. From the maroon, cut the top saddle. From the navy, cut the bottom saddle blanket. From the navy print, cut the front and back decorative harnesses. From the scrap of black, cut the hooves.

SEWING INSTRUCTIONS:

Cut the backing fabric the same size as the front and baste to the wrong side. Trace all stitching lines onto the appliqués with the dressmaker's carbon paper. Using the photo as a guide, position the appliqués onto the front and baste. Keeping the bias tape folded, baste it onto the bridle lines and straight stitch it. Machine zigzag around the edges of the appliqués first and then do the details as follows. Use gray thread on the white tail, black for the eyelid and nostril, and navy on the saddle. Use matching threads for the rest. Clip all threads and remove the bastings from the appliqués.

Sew the border strips together and press seams. Sew a white border strip to each side and then to the top and bottom. Now sew the widest mauve print border to the top and bottom only. Remember to press after sewing on each border. Next sew the narrower mauve print border to each side first and then to the top and bottom again. Press the whole quilt front. Sew the quilt front to the quilt back and batt by referring to the general instructions. Baste all three layers together. Machine quilt around the pony, on both edges of the white borders, and on the outside edges of the wider mauve print borders at the top and bottom. Remove bastings.

1 square = 1"

COWS

Add a country theme to the nursery with these black and white Holsteins.

Finished size is 34" x 43 1/2"

FABRIC REQUIREMENTS:

2 yards medium blue
3/4 yard white
3/8 yard green and white print
3/8 yard blue and white print
1/8 yard black
5/8 yard backing fabric
a scrap of pink
39" x 48 1/2" quilt batt
Thread: pink, black, green, white, and blue

CUTTING INSTRUCTIONS:

From the medium blue, cut border strips 4 1/2" wide by 4 3/8 yards long and cut the back 39" x 48 1/2". From the white, cut border strips 1 3/4" wide by 6 yards long and cut 6 cows. From the green and white print, cut six grass sections. From the blue and white print, cut 6 sky sections. From the black, cut six sets of spots for the cows. From the pink, cut six udders. From the backing fabric, cut six rectangles 10 3/4" x 11 3/4". Trace all stitching lines onto the cows with the dressmaker's carbon paper.

SEWING INSTRUCTIONS:

Using the photo as a guide, arrange the appliqués onto the rectangles cut from the backing fabric, and baste them in place. Machine zigzag around the edges of the appliqués first and then do the details as follows. Use black thread for the cows and spots, pink for the udders, and green between the sky and grass sections. Clip all threads and remove bastings from the appliqués.

Sew the border strips together and press seams. Join the two top cows together by sewing on a white border strip between them. Do the same for the middle and bottom pairs of cows. Now join the top section to the middle section by sewing on a white border between them. Do the same for the middle section and bottom section. Remember to press after sewing on each border. Sew a white border to each side and then the top and bottom. Do the same with the medium blue borders. Press the whole quilt front. Sew the quilt front to the quilt back and batt by referring to the general instructions. Baste all three layers together. Machine quilt around each cow, and on both edges of the white borders. Remove bastings.

1 square = 1″

HEARTS

These two-toned hearts are tied up with pretty green bows.

Finished size is 34 1/2″ x 42 1/2″

FABRIC REQUIREMENTS:

1 3/4 yards medium green
3/4 yard red print
3/4 yard white
3/8 yard pink
7/8 yard backing fabric
39 1/2″ x 47 1/2″ quilt batt
Thread: light green, pink, red, and
    medium green

CUTTING INSTRUCTIONS:

From the medium green, cut border strips
1 1/2″ wide by 4 1/2 yards long. Cut the back
39 1/2″ x 47 1/2″ and cut four green bows
and ribbons. From the red print, cut border
strips 2 1/4″ wide by 8 1/8 yards long. Cut
four bottom heart sections. From the white,
cut four 13 1/2″ squares for the fronts. From
the pink, cut four top heart sections and a
border strip 3 1/4″ wide by 32″ long.

SEWING INSTRUCTIONS:

Cut four 13 1/2″ squares from the backing
fabric and baste to the wrong sides of the
fronts. Trace the stitching lines onto the bows
and ribbons with the dressmaker's carbon
paper. Using the photo as a guide, position
the appliqués onto the quilt fronts and baste.
Machine zigzag around the edges of the appliqués first and then do the details as
follows. Use light green thread for the bows
and ribbons and matching thread for the
heart sections. Clip all threads and remove
bastings from the appliqués.

Sew the border strips together and press
seams. Sew on a red print border between
the two top squares. Do the same for the two
bottom squares. Now sew a red print border
across the bottom of the top section. Do the
same across the top of the bottom section.
Join the top to the bottom by sewing on the
pink border. Remember to press seams after
sewing on each border section. Next sew a
red print border across the top and across the
bottom. Still using the red print border sew a
border on each side first and then across the
top and bottom again. Sew on the medium
green borders sides first and then top and
bottom. Press the whole quilt front. Sew the
quilt front to the quilt back and batt by referring to the general instructions. Baste all
three layers together. Machine quilt around
the hearts and on both edges of the red print
borders. Remove bastings.

1 square = 1"

UNDER THE SEA

The little mermaid lives in her sand castle under the sea.

Finished size is 33 1/2" x 43"

FABRIC REQUIREMENTS:

1 5/8 yards peach
3/8 yard white
7/8 yard sea green
1/4 yard tan
1/8 yard green and white dot
a scrap of medium green and white
    stripe, brown, navy, peach and white
    print, medium green, and yellow
1 yard backing fabric
38 1/2" x 48" quilt batt
Thread: brown, medium green, coral,
    navy, peach, tan, white, and pink

CUTTING INSTRUCTIONS:

From the peach, cut border strips 2" wide by 4 3/4 yards long. Cut the back 38 1/2" x 48". Also cut face, neck, and arms of the mermaid. From the white, cut border strips 2 1/4" wide by 4 1/4" yards long. From the sea green, cut the front 27 1/2" x 37 1/2". From the tan, cut the sand castle. From the green and white dot, cut the mermaid's bottom section. Using the scraps cut the following: sea horse from the navy, shell and star fish from the peach and white print, mermaid's top, and two flags from the green and white stripe, mermaid's hair from the brown, fish from the yellow, and two plants from the medium green.

SEWING INSTRUCTIONS:

Cut the backing fabric the same size as the front and baste to the wrong side. Trace all stitching lines onto the appliqués with the dressmaker's carbon paper. Also trace the sand lines onto the quilt front. Using the photo as a guide, position appliqués onto the quilt front and baste. Machine zigzag around the edges of the appliqués first and then do the details as follows. Use brown thread on the castle, green on the fish, and coral on the shell and starfish. Use matching threads on the rest. Stitch over the sand lines with tan thread. Use a very narrow brown stitch for the mermaid's eyes, eyebrows, nose, and finger details. Use pink thread for the mouth. Stitch a white eye on the sea-horse. Clip all threads and remove the bastings from the appliqués.

Sew the border strips together and press seams. Sew on the white borders doing the sides first and then top and bottom. Remember to press seams after sewing on each border section. Now do the same with the peach borders. Press the whole quilt front. Sew the quilt front to the quilt back and batt by referring to the general instructions. Baste all three layers together. Machine quilt around each appliqué along the sand lines, and on both edges of the white border. Remove bastings.

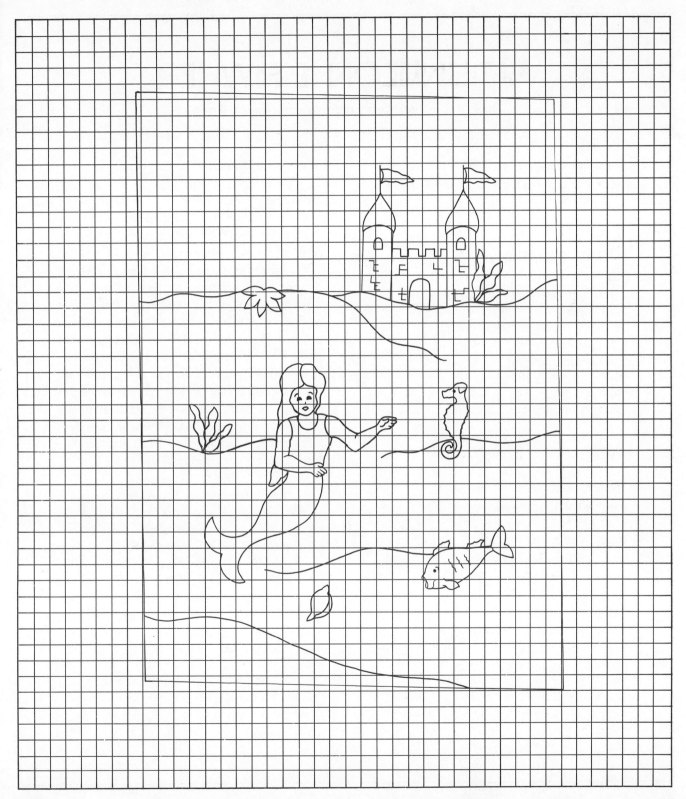

1 square = 1"

WATERMELON PINWHEEL

Bright red watermelon slices make a colorful pinwheel.

Finished size is 36 1/2" x 46"

FABRIC REQUIREMENTS:

2 yards green and white stripe
1 yard white
1/4 yard medium green
1/4 yard red
1 yard backing fabric
41 1/2" x 51" quilt batt
Thread: white, dark green, red, light
    green, and black

CUTTING INSTRUCTIONS:

From the green and white stripe, cut individual strips which, when sewn together, will form one border 4 1/2" wide by 4 3/4 yards long, and cut the back 41 1/2" x 51". From the white, cut twelve 10" squares for the front. From the medium green, cut fourteen watermelon rinds. From the red, cut fourteen watermelon slices.

SEWING INSTRUCTIONS:

From the backing fabric, cut twelve 10" squares and baste them to the wrong sides of the fronts. Sew the front squares together in rows of three to make one whole front (be sure to press after sewing each seam). Using the photo as a guide, position watermelons onto the front about 1/8" from the seams and baste. Machine zigzag the watermelons using dark green for the outside rind, light green for the inside rind, and red for the top of the watermelon. Stitch in the seeds with black thread by starting with the stitch width control knob on very narrow, and turning it to wider as you stitch. Do them in different sizes at random. Clip all threads and remove the bastings from the appliqués.

Sew the border strips together and press seams. Sew on the green and white stripe borders doing the sides first and then the top and bottom. After sewing remember to press each border section. Next, sew the quilt front to the quilt back and batt by referring to the general instructions. Baste all three layers together. Machine quilt around each watermelon and on the inside edge of the green and white striped border. Remove bastings.

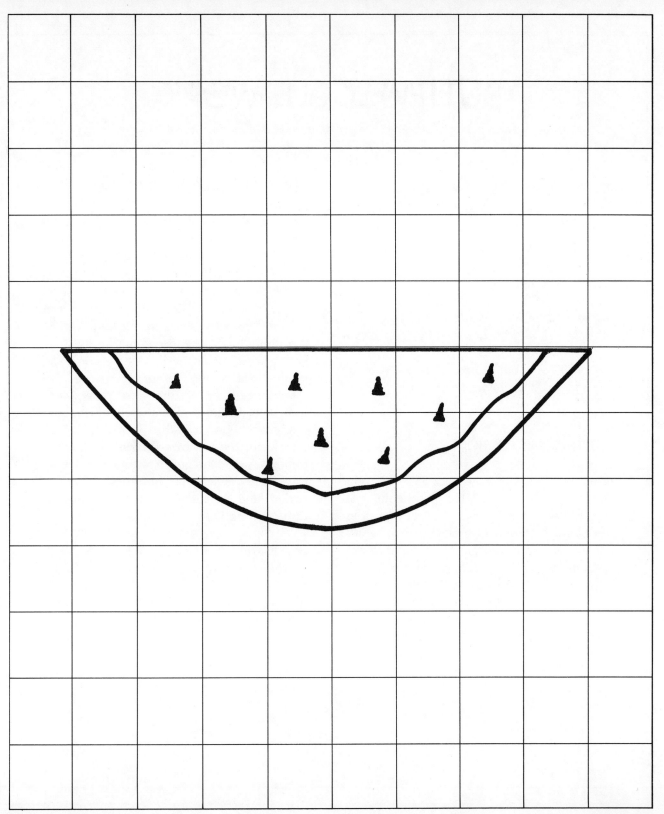

BUTTERFLY CUT WORK

Delicate cutwork butterflies on a pale yellow background are framed with eyelet lace.

Finished size is 33 1/2" x 43"

FABRIC REQUIREMENTS:

2 3/8 yards yellow
1/2 yard white
4 3/4 yards of 2 1/2" wide white eyelet lace
4 yards of 1/4" wide green satin picot ribbon
1 yard backing fabric
38" x 48" quilt batt (1 yard fusible webbing)
Thread: green, white, and yellow

CUTTING INSTRUCTIONS:

From the yellow, cut the back 38" x 48" and the front 34" x 43 1/2". From the white, cut two butterflies as follows. Steam the fusible webbing to the wrong side of the white fabric. Just hold the iron above it and steam it until the webbing adheres to the fabric. Now trace half of the butterfly onto the white fabric. Fold the fabric on the center of the butterfly and pin together. Cut out the butterfly from both layers. This way both sides will be the same.

SEWING INSTRUCTIONS:

Sew the white eyelet lace around the quilt front so that the scallopy edge of the lace is 3/8" in from the edge of the quilt front. Machine zigzag the inside raw edge and use a straight stitch for the outside edge. First sew on the sides, then sew on the top and bottom extending the ends to the edges of the quilt. To miter the corners, draw lines with a pencil and ruler from the inside edge of the lace to the corner. Trim lace and machine zigzag on the line. Now, with matching thread and a straight stitch, sew the green ribbon over the inside edge of the lace. Using the photo as a guide, position the butterflies onto the quilt front and press them into place. With white thread machine zigzag around the cut edges of the butterflies. Clip all threads.

Sew the quilt front to the quilt back and batt by referring to the general instructions. Be careful not to stitch over the scallopy edges of the lace. Baste all three layers together. Machine quilt around the butterflies and along the inside edge of the green ribbon. Remove bastings.

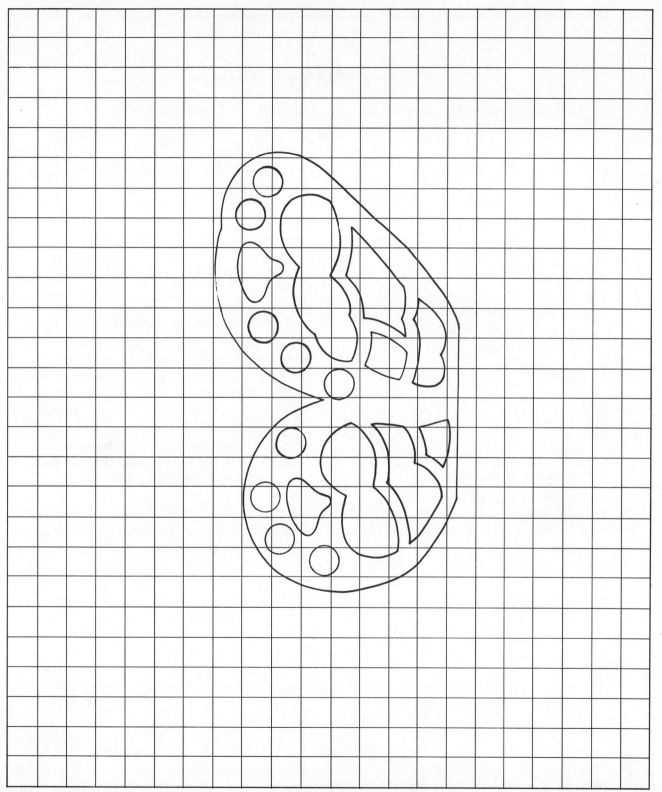

1 square = 1″

BABY

Make this quilt more personal by appliquéing baby's name in place of BABY.

Finished size is 35 1/2" x 41"

FABRIC REQUIREMENTS:

2 3/8 yards cream print
3/4 yard salmon
1/4 yard tan
a scrap of sea green, lavender, medium
　blue, pink, black, and light gray
5/8 yard backing fabric
41" x 47" quilt batt
Thread: cream, salmon, tan, gray, sea
　green, lavender, medium blue, pink,
　and black

CUTTING INSTRUCTIONS:

From the cream print, cut border strips 3 1/2"
wide by 4 1/8 yards long. Cut the back 41" x
47" and cut the front 21 1/2" x 27 1/2". From
the salmon, cut the first border strips 3 1/2"
wide by 3 1/2 yards long. Cut the third border
strips 2 3/4" wide by 4 5/8 yards long. Also
cut the B and the second paint splotch. From
the tan, cut the pallet and the brush's handle. Cut the A and the first and fifth paint
splotch from the sea green. Cut the B and the
third paint splotch from the lavender. Cut the
Y, the paint on the brush and the sixth paint
splotch from the medium blue. Cut the fourth

paint splotch from the pink. Cut the brush's
bristles from the black. Cut the brush's ferrule from the light gray.

SEWING INSTRUCTIONS:

Cut the backing fabric the same size as the
front and baste to the wrong side. Trace the
stitching lines onto the appliqués with the
dressmaker's carbon paper. Using the photo
as a guide, position the appliqués onto the
front and baste. Machine zigzag around the
edges of the appliqués first and then do the
details as follows. Use matching thread on
all of the appliqués. Use a narrower stitch for
the details of the ferrule. Clip threads and
remove the bastings from the appliqués.

Sew the border strips together and press
seams. Sew on the wider salmon borders doing the sides first and then top and bottom.
Remember to press the seams after sewing
on each border section. Now do the same
with the cream print and narrower salmon
borders in the same order. Press the whole
quilt front. Sew the quilt front to the quilt
back and batt by referring to the general instructions. Baste all three layers together.
Machine quilt around the appliqués and on
the inside edges of all three borders.
Remove bastings.

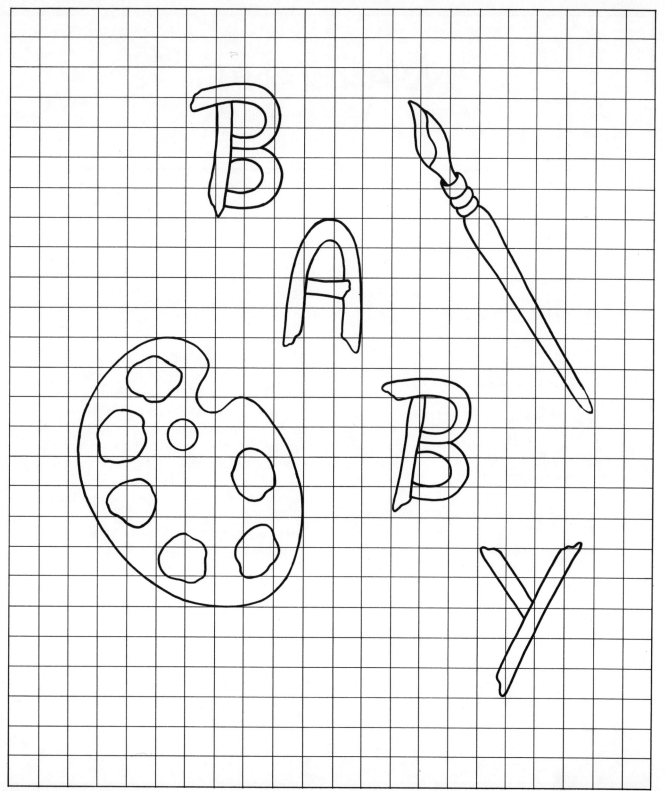

1 square = 1"

INDIAN BLANKET

Make this Indian design quilt for your little papoose.

Finished size is 35" x 44"

FABRIC REQUIREMENTS:

2 1/2 yards of tan
1/2 yard white
1/8 yard lavender
1/8 yard light blue
1/8 yard yellow
1/8 yard pink
1/8 yard light green
1 yard backing fabric
40" x 49" quilt batt
Thread: white and tan

CUTTING INSTRUCTIONS:

From the tan, cut the back 40" x 49" and the front 35 1/2" x 44 1/2". From the white, cut two white border appliqués by placing the center on the fold of the fabric. Also cut nine small diamonds. From the lavender, cut four #1 arrow sections and two large diamonds. From the light blue, cut four #2 arrow sections and two large diamonds. From the yellow, cut four #3 arrow sections and one large diamond. From the pink, cut four #4 arrow sections and two large diamonds. From the green, cut four #5 arrow sections and two large diamonds.

SEWING INSTRUCTIONS:

Cut the backing fabric the same size as the front and baste to the wrong side. Using the photo as a guide, position appliqués onto the quilt front and baste. Machine zigzag the appliqués using white thread for all of them and a wider stitch width. Clip all threads and remove all the bastings from the appliqués.

Sew quilt front to the quilt back and batt by referring to the general instructions. Baste all three layers together. Machine quilt around all of the appliqués. Remove bastings.

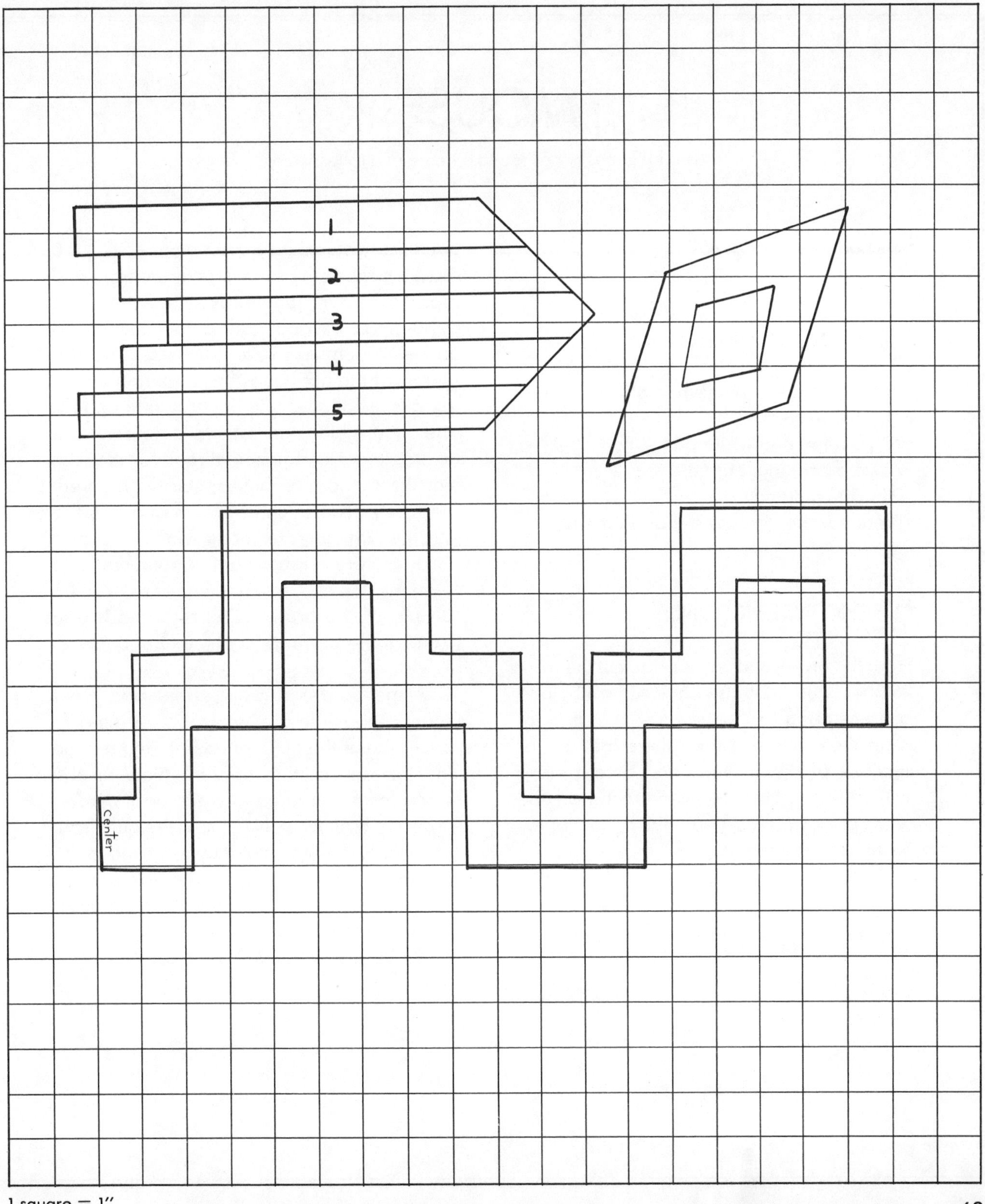

1 square = 1″

MOUSE

This little mouse has found a home in a roller skate.

Finished size is 35" x 45"

FABRIC REQUIREMENTS:

2 5/8 yards green and white print
3/4 yard white
1/8 yard tan and white print
7/8 yard backing fabric
40" x 50" quilt batt
Thread: white, tan, green, and brown

CUTTING INSTRUCTIONS:

From the green and white print, cut the front 26 3/4" x 36 1/2", the back 40" x 50", and border strips 3 1/2" wide x 4 5/8 yards long. From the white, cut the rollerskate, center sections of the wheels, and border strips 1 3/4" wide x 4 yards long. From the tan and white print, cut the wheels, the bottom of the skate, and the mouse.

SEWING INSTRUCTIONS:

Trace all stitching lines onto the appliqués with the dressmaker's carbon paper. Cut the backing fabric the same size as the front and baste to the wrong side. Using the photo as a guide, position appliqués onto the front and baste. Machine zigzag stitch around the edges of the appliqués first and then do the details as follows. Use the brown thread for the mouse, the tan for the details on the skate, and use matching thread for the rest. For the eye of the mouse, start with a very narrow zigzag stitch of brown and turn the stitch width control knob to wider, and then back to very narrow again as you sew. To highlight the eye, sew a few stitches of white on top of the brown. Clip all threads and remove the bastings from the appliqués.

Sew the border strips together and press seams. Next, sew a white border strip to each side of the quilt, press flat, and sew on the top and bottom borders. Now do the same for the green and white print border. Press the quilt front. Next, sew the quilt front to the quilt back and batt by referring to the general instructions. Baste the three layers together. Machine quilt around the mouse, rollerskate, and along each edge of the white border. Remove bastings.

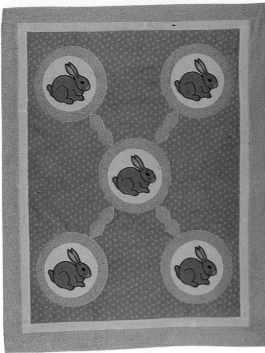

Bunnies

Duck

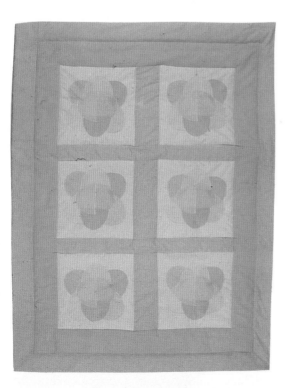

Pastel Geometric

Bell Flowers

Bluebirds

Dalmatian

Spring Flowers

Toy Shelf

Farm Scene

Unicorn

Sunflowers

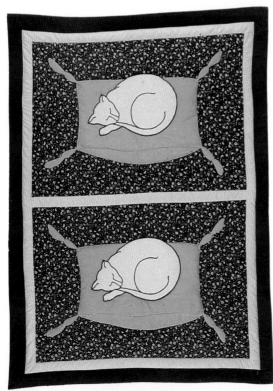

Sleepy Cats

Carousel Pony

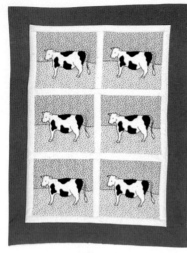

Cows

Hearts

Under the Sea

Watermelon Pinwheel

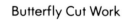

Butterfly Cut Work

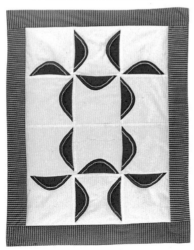

Baby

Indian Blanket

Mouse

Kittens

Teddy Bears

Frog Pond

Parrot

Easter Bunny

Whales

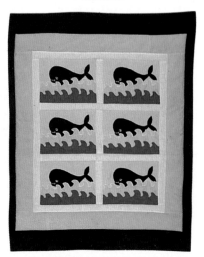

Penguin

Gingerbread Boys & Girls

Clown

Pink Flamingos

Balloons

Picture Frame

Basket of Pansies

Toy Soldier

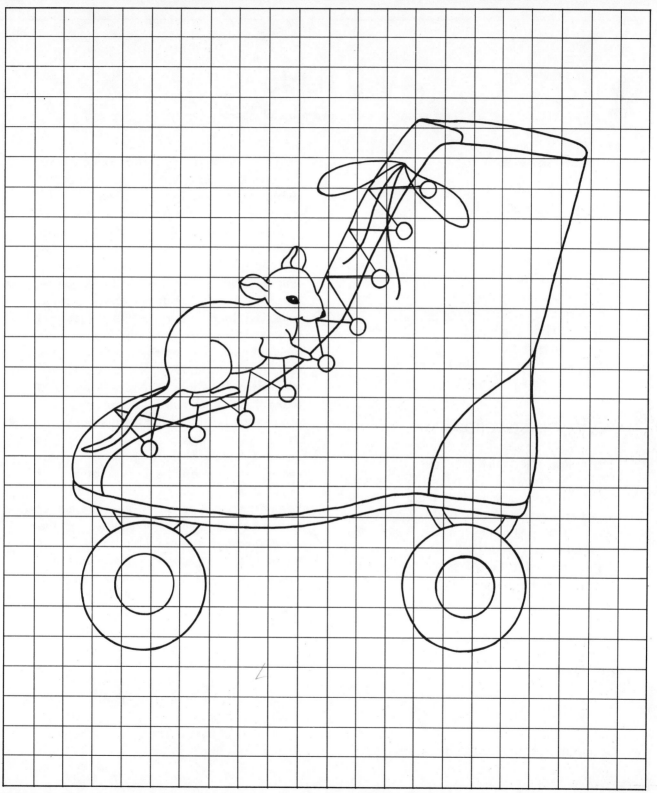

1 square = 1"

KITTENS

These naughty kittens have been licking the batter.

Finished size is 35'' x 46''

FABRIC REQUIREMENTS:

2 1/4 yards butterscotch print
1 1/4 yards white
1/4 yard black
1/4 yard medium blue
a scrap of pink and light green
7/8 yard backing fabric
40'' x 51'' quilt batt
Thread: white, blue, black, pink, and
    light green

CUTTING INSTRUCTIONS:

From the butterscotch print, cut border strips 1 3/4'' wide by 6 1/8 yards long. Cut the back 40'' x 51'' and cut four bowls. From the white, cut border strips 2'' wide by 2 1/2 yards long for the sides. For the top and bottom, cut border strips 4'' wide by 2 1/4 yards long. Cut four rectangles 14 1/4'' x 17 1/2'' for the front. Also cut four sets of cheeks. From the black, cut four kittens and four sets of pupils. From the blue, cut four sets of stripes for the bowls. From the pink, cut four noses and four tongues. From the light green, cut four sets of eyes.

SEWING INSTRUCTIONS:

Trace all stitching lines onto the appliqués with the dressmaker's carbon paper. From the backing fabric, cut four rectangles the same size as the fronts and baste to the wrong side. Using the photo as a guide, position the appliqués onto the fronts and baste. Machine zigzag around the edges of the appliqués first, and then do the details as follows. With a narrower stitch, use white thread for the inside stitching lines on the kittens. Use blue thread for the stripes and outline of the bowls. Use black thread for the white cheeks. Use matching thread for the rest. After appliquéing the eye sections, stitch across the tops with white thread to make them stand out. Clip all threads and remove the bastings from the appliqués.

Sew the border strips together and press seams. To sew on the butterscotch print borders, start with the center border between the top kittens and then the center border between the bottom kittens. Join the top and bottom kittens with a border across the middle. Next, sew a border on each side and then do the top and bottom. Be sure to press seams after sewing on each border section. Sew a white narrower border to each side, and the white wider border to the top and bottom. Press the whole quilt front. Then, sew the quilt front to the quilt back and batt by referring to the general instructions. Baste the three layers together. Machine quilt around each bowl and kitten, and on both edges of the butterscotch print borders. Remove bastings.

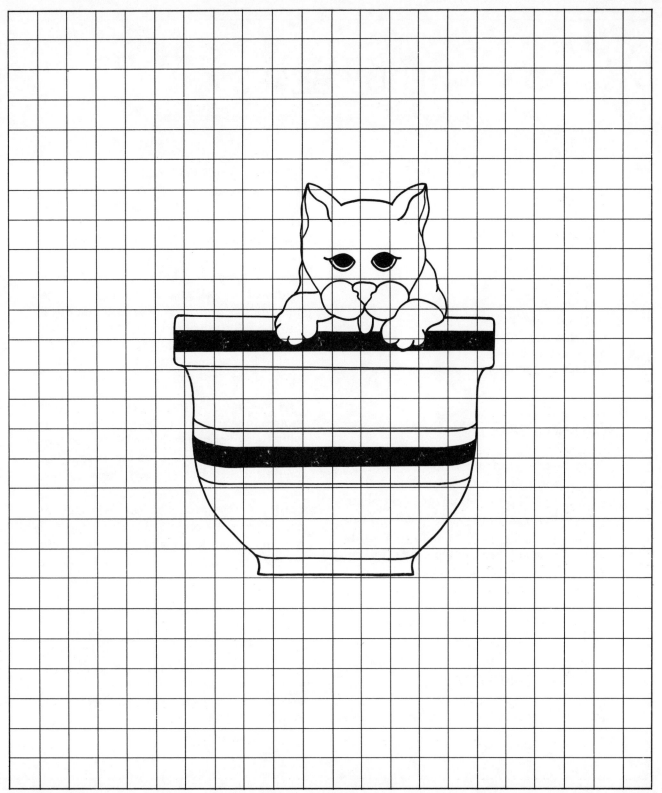

1 square = 1"

TEDDY BEARS

Every child loves teddy bears. Make these in denim and calico.

Finished size is 38" x 43"

FABRIC REQUIREMENTS:

1 7/8 yards red print
1 yard white
1 yard denim
   a scrap of black
3/4 yard backing fabric
43" x 48" quilt batt
Thread: white and red

CUTTING INSTRUCTIONS:

From the white, cut four rectangles 12" x 15" for the front, and cut border strips 1 3/4" wide by 4 1/8 yards long. From the denim, cut four teddy bears (two facing left and two facing right). Also cut border strips 4" wide by 4 5/8 yards long. From the red print, cut paws, feet, snouts, and centers of ears. Also cut border strips 1 3/4" wide by 5 3/8 yards long and cut the back 43" x 48". From the scrap of black, cut the noses and eyes.

SEWING INSTRUCTIONS:

Trace all stitching lines onto the appliqués with the dressmaker's carbon paper. From the backing fabric, cut four rectangles the same size as the fronts and baste to the wrong sides. Using the photo as a guide, position the appliqués onto the fronts and baste. Machine zigzag stitch around the edges of the appliqués first and then do the details as follows. Use white thread for the nose, mouth, and eyes. Use red thread on all the rest. Clip all threads and remove the bastings from the appliqués.

Sew the border strips together and press seams. To sew on the red print borders, start with the center border between the top teddy bears and then the center border between the two bottom teddy bears. Now, join the top and bottom teddy bears with a border across the middle. Next, sew a border on each side and then do the top and bottom. Be sure to press seams after sewing on each border section. Sew on the white and denim borders doing the sides first and then the top and bottom. Press the whole quilt front. Next sew the quilt front to the quilt back and batt by referring to the general instructions. Baste the three layers together. Machine quilt around each teddy bear, on both edges of the red print borders, and on the outside edge of the white border. Remove bastings.

1 square = 1"

FROG POND

The water lilies are blooming on the frog pond.

Finished size is 34 1/2" x 43 1/2"

FABRIC REQUIREMENTS:

2 1/2 yards dark green print
3/4 yard light blue
1/4 yard medium green
1/4 yard light gray
1/8 yard light green
1/8 yard pink
a scrap of yellow
1 yard backing fabric
39 1/2" x 48 1/2" quilt batt
Thread: all three shades of green, gray,
   light blue, yellow, and rose

CUTTING INSTRUCTIONS:

From the dark green print, cut the front 35" x 44" and the back 39 1/2" x 48 1/2". From the light blue, cut the pond. From the medium green, cut three frogs. From the light gray, cut three large rocks and three small rocks. From the light green, cut six small and five large lily pads. From the pink, cut eight lilies. From the yellow, cut eight centers for the lilies.

SEWING INSTRUCTIONS:

Trace all stitching lines onto the appliqués with the dressmaker's carbon paper. Cut the backing fabric the same size as the front and baste to the wrong side. Using the photo as a guide, position the appliqués onto the front and baste. Machine zigzag stitch around the edges of the appliqués first and then do the details as follows. Stitch the pond first. Use the rose thread on the pink lilies so the petals will stand out. Use matching thread on all the rest. Clip all the threads and remove the bastings from the appliqués.

Press the whole quilt front. Next, sew the quilt front to the quilt back and batt by referring to the general instructions. Baste the three layers together. Machine quilt around each appliqué and the edge of the pond. Remove bastings.

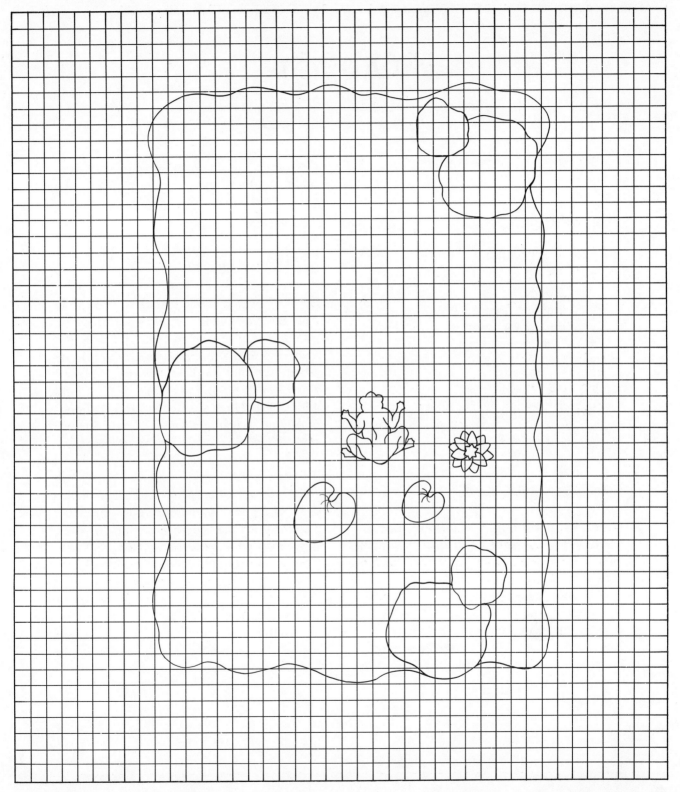

1 square = 1"

PARROT

The bright-colored parrot has a vine growing around his ring.

Finished size is 33 1/2" x 43 1/2"

FABRIC REQUIREMENTS:

2 1/8 yards yellow print
7/8 yard white
1/4 yard orange
1/4 yard medium green
1/8 yard dark green print
a scrap of yellow and black
5/8 yard backing fabric
38 1/2" x 48 1/2" quilt batt
Thread: dark green, medium green,
    yellow, white, orange, black, and
    dark tan

CUTTING INSTRUCTIONS:

From the yellow print, cut border strips 5"
wide by 4 1/2 yards long and the back
38 1/2" x 48 1/2". From the white, cut the
front 19 1/2" x 29 1/2" and border strips
1 3/4" wide by 3 5/8 yards long. From the
orange, cut the border strips 1 1/2" wide by
3 1/4 yards long and the parrot's face and
top wing section. From the medium green,
cut the parrot. From the dark green print, cut
the leaves. From the yellow, cut the parrot's
beak, middle wing section, and foot. Cut the
eye from the black.

SEWING INSTRUCTIONS:

Cut the backing fabric the same size as the
front and baste to the wrong side. Using the
photo as a guide, trace the circle onto the
front and position and baste appliqués into
place. With the dark tan thread, machine
zigzag stitch around the circle using a little
wider stitch. Now, stitch around all the appliqués with matching thread. Clip all threads
and remove bastings from the appliqués.

Sew the border strips together and press
seams. Sew the borders onto the front in the
order of orange, white, and yellow print. Do
the sides first then top and bottom pressing
after each one. Press the whole quilt front.
Now sew the quilt front to the quilt back and
batt by referring to the general instructions.
Baste the three layers together. Machine
quilt around the outside edge of the ring, the
parrot, the leaves, both edges of the orange
border, and the outside edge of the white
border. Remove bastings.

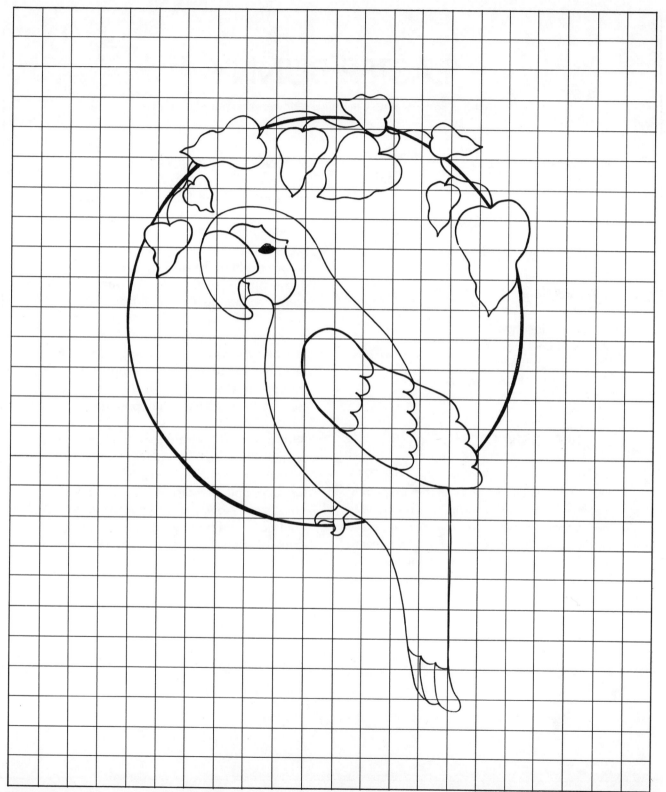

1 square = 1"

EASTER BUNNY

A white Easter bunny with delicate flowers and pastel eggs.

Finished size is 34" x 44"

FABRIC REQUIREMENTS:

2 1/4 yards lavender print
7/8 yard white
1/8 yard green
1/8 yard pink
a scrap of lavender
7/8 yard backing fabric
39" x 49" quilt batt
Thread: pink, lavender, and green

CUTTING INSTRUCTIONS:

From the lavender print, cut the front 29" x 38" and the back 39" x 49". From the white, cut the bunny and individual strips which, sewn together, will form one border 3 1/4" wide by 4 1/2 yards long. From the green, cut the grasses. From the pink, cut the bunny's nose, ear section, flowers, and two eggs. From the lavender, cut two eggs.

SEWING INSTRUCTIONS:

Trace all stitching lines onto the applique with the dressmaker's carbon paper. Cut the backing fabric the same size as the front and baste to the wrong side. Using the photo as a guide, position the appliqués onto the front and baste. Trace the flower stems with the carbon paper to the quilt front. Machine zigzag stitch around the edge of the appliqués first and then do the details as follows. Stitch on the stem lines using green thread. Use pink thread on the bunny and matching thread for the rest. Clip all threads and remove bastings from the appliqués.

Sew the border strips together and press seams. Next, sew a white border to each side of the front and press, then sew on the top and bottom borders. Press the whole quilt front. Now sew the quilt front to the quilt back and batt by referring to the general instructions. Baste the three layers together. Machine quilt around all the appliqués and along the inside edge of the white border. Remove bastings.

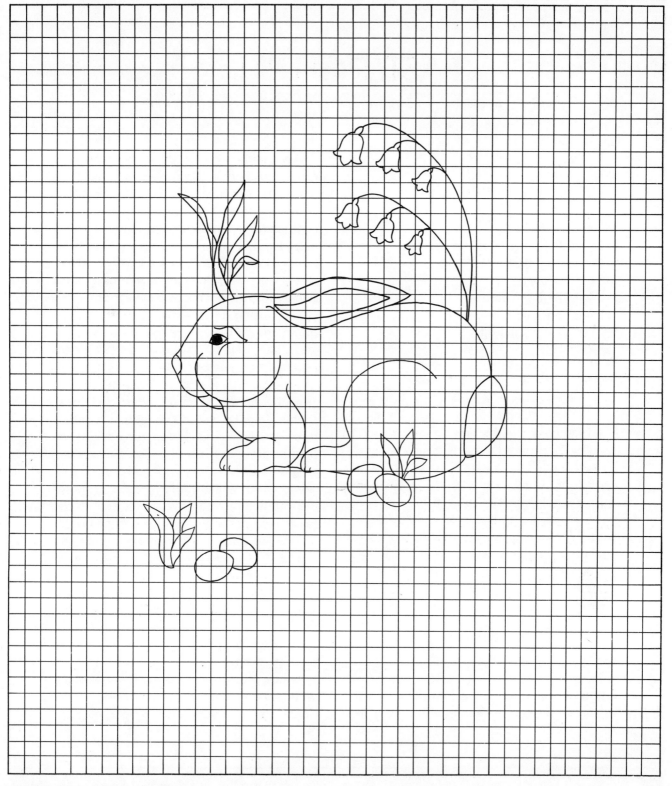

1 square = 1"

WHALES

The whales are floating on the ocean waves.

Finished size is 34 1/2" x 43"

FABRIC REQUIREMENTS:

1 3/4 yards navy
5/8 yard light blue dotted swiss
1/2 yard light blue
3/8 yard white
1/4 yard medium blue
1/2 yard backing fabric
39 1/2" x 48" quilt batt
Thread: white, medium blue, and navy

CUTTING INSTRUCTIONS:

From the navy, cut the side border strips 2" wide by 2 1/4 yards long, and cut the top and bottom border strips 4 1/2" wide by 2 1/4 yards long. Cut the back 39 1/2" x 48" and cut six whales. From the light blue dotted swiss, cut border strips 3 3/4" wide by 3 3/4 yards long and cut six top waves. From the light blue, cut six rectangles 8 1/4" x 10 3/4" for the fronts. From the white, cut border strips 1 3/4" wide by 5 1/2 yards long. From the medium blue, cut six bottom waves.

SEWING INSTRUCTIONS:

Cut the backing fabric the same size as the fronts and baste to the wrong sides. Trace on the whales' mouths and eyes with the dressmaker's carbon paper. Using the photo as a guide, position the appliqués onto the fronts and baste. Machine zigzag around the edges of the appliqués first and then do the details as follows. Use navy thread on the whales' outlines. Use white thread on the top waves and matching thread on the bottom waves. Use a narrower stitch for the whales' mouths and eyebrows in white. Do the eyes in white as well, using a wider stitch to start and turn the stitch width control knob to narrower as you stitch. Clip all threads and remove the bastings from the appliqués.

Sew the border strips together and press seams. Join the two top rectangles together by sewing on a white border between them. Do the same for the middle and bottom rectangles. Join the top section to the middle by sewing on a white border. Do the same for the middle and bottom sections. Remember to press seams after sewing on each border section. Sew a white border to each side and then do the top and bottom. Next sew on the dotted swiss border in the same order. Sew the narrower navy border to each side and the wider to the top and bottom. Press the whole quilt front. Sew the quilt front to the quilt back and batt by referring to the general instructions. Baste all three layers together. Machine quilt on both edges of the white borders and on the outside edge of the dotted swiss border. Remove bastings.

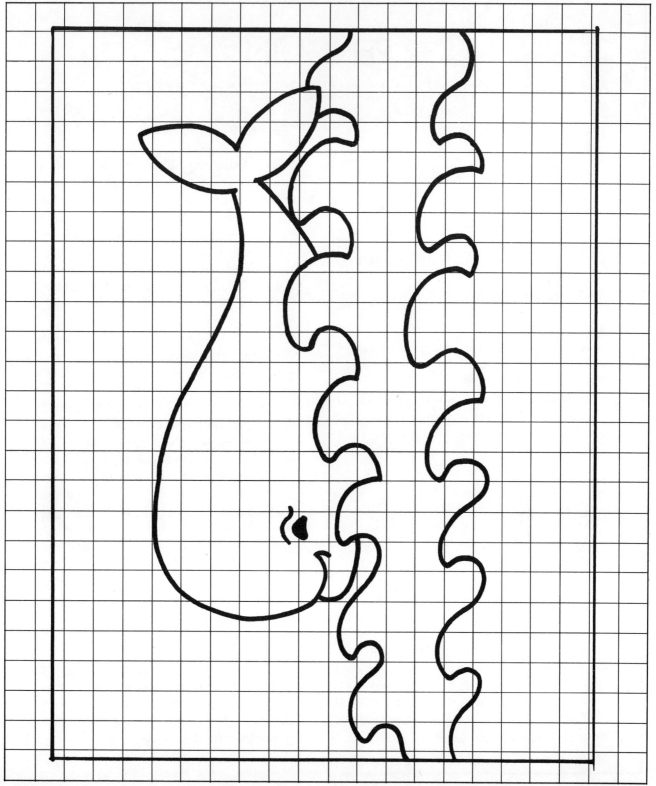

1 square = 1"

PENGUIN

The penguin stays warm while sliding about in his argyle sweater vest.

Finished size is 34" x 43 1/2"

FABRIC REQUIREMENTS:

2 1/4 yards of light blue with white dots
3/4 yard white
1/2 yard dark green
1/8 yard tan
1/8 yard black
a scrap of navy and yellow
3/4 yard backing fabric
39" x 48 1/2" quilt batt
Thread: black, light blue, navy, yellow,
    brown, white, and dark green

CUTTING INSTRUCTIONS:

From the light blue dot, cut border strips 4"
wide x 4 3/8 yards long. Cut the back 39" x
50" and cut the sky section. From the white,
cut the snowy hills and one eye. From the
dark green, cut border strips 1 3/4" wide by
3 7/8 yards long. Cut the penguin's sweater
vest, two large trees, and one small tree.
From the tan, cut the sled. From the black,
cut the penguin's head, wings, and feet.
From the scraps of navy and yellow, cut the
diamonds on the sweater vest (2 yellow and
1 navy). Cut the backing fabric 25" x 36".

SEWING INSTRUCTIONS:

Trace all stitching lines onto the appliqués
with dressmaker's carbon paper. Place the
snowy hills and sky sections onto the backing
fabric and baste. Using the photo as a guide,
trace the penguin's lower body and neck
outlines directly onto the front. Do the same
for the sled runners and rope handle. Now
position all the appliqués onto the front and
baste. Machine zigzag around the edges of
the appliqués first and then do the details as
follows. Use white thread on the sweater
vest, light blue on the hills, brown for the
sled, black on all of the penguin including
the eye, and matching thread on the trees
and diamonds. Use a very narrow stitch for
the ribbing on the sweater vest and the X's
on the diamonds. Use navy thread for the X
on the yellow diamonds and yellow for the X
on the navy diamond. With black thread,
stitch in the center of the eye. Clip all threads
and remove all bastings from the appliqués.

Sew the border strips together and press
seams. Sew on the green borders doing the
sides first and then the top and bottom.
Remember to press seams after sewing on
each border section. Do the same with the
blue dot borders. Press the whole quilt front.
Next, sew the quilt front to the quilt back and
batt by referring to the general instructions.
Baste all three layers together. Machine quilt
along the tops of each hill, around the sled,
penguins, trees, and on both edges of the
green border. Remove bastings.

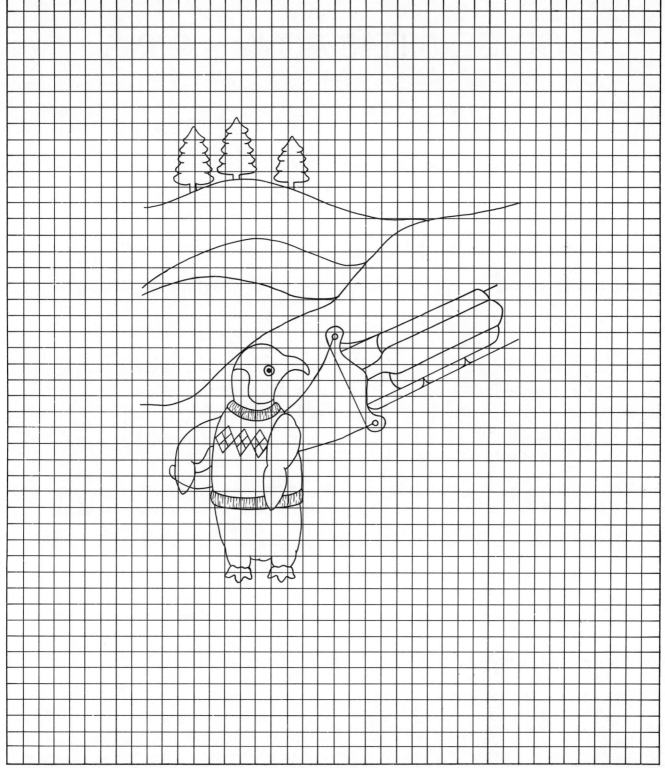

1 square = 1"

GINGERBREAD BOYS & GIRLS

The gingerbread boys and girls are dressed for play in their green corduroy outfits.

Finished size is 35 1/2" x 44"

FABRIC REQUIREMENTS:

2 1/2 yards green corduroy
3/8 yard red and green plaid
3/8 yard off white
1/4 yard brown
3/8 yard backing fabric
40 1/2" x 49" quilt batt
Thread: white, brown, and green

CUTTING INSTRUCTIONS:

From the green corduroy, cut border strips 2 1/2" wide by 2 3/8 yards long for the sides. Cut border strips 4 3/4" wide by 2 1/8 yards long for the top and bottom. Also cut three rectangles 10" x 13 3/4", cut the back 40 1/2" x 49", cut three girls' jumpers, and three boys' coveralls. From the red and green plaid, cut border strips 2" wide by 6 5/8 yards long. From the brown, cut 3 boys and 3 girls. From the off white, cut three rectangles 10" x 13 3/4" for the fronts.

SEWING INSTRUCTIONS:

From the backing fabric, cut three rectangles the same size as the fronts and baste to the wrong sides. Transfer all stitching lines to the appliqués with the dressmaker's carbon paper. Using the photo as a guide, position the appliqués on the fronts and baste. Machine zigzag around the edges of the appliqués first and then do the details as follows. Stitch the edges of the gingerbread boys and girls in brown first, and then stitch very close to the brown stitching with a narrower white stitch. Also use this narrower white stitch for the hair and faces. Use green thread on the clothes and white for the buttons. Clip all threads and remove bastings from the appliqués.

Sew the border strips together and press seams. Join the top appliquéd rectangle to the green corduroy rectangle by sewing on a plaid border strip between them. Referring to the photo, do the same for the middle and bottom rectangles alternating the off white and green. Join the top section to the middle section by sewing a plaid border crosswise. Do the same for the middle and bottom sections. Remember to press seams after sewing on each border section. Sew a plaid border to each side, top, and bottom. Using the narrower green corduroy, sew a border onto each side. With the wider green corduroy, sew on a border to the top and bottom. Press the whole quilt front. Sew the quilt front to the quilt back and batt by referring to the general instructions. Baste all three layers together. Machine quilt around the boys and girls and on both edges of the plaid borders. Remove bastings.

1 square = 1″

CLOWN

A cheerful clown floating through the air on his umbrella.

Finished size is 35 1/2″ x 46″

FABRIC REQUIREMENTS:

2 1/4 yards brown with white pin stripes
7/8 yard white
1/4 yard pink with white dots
1/4 yard orchid print
1/8 yard flesh
a scrap of yellow, purple, hot pink, and
   orchid and white stripe
7/8 yard backing fabric
40 1/2″ x 51″ quilt batt
Thread: pink, brown, orchid, flesh, purple,
   yellow, and white

CUTTING INSTRUCTIONS:

From the brown pin stripe, cut individual strips which, when sewn together, will form one border 4″ wide by 4 5/8 yards long. Cut the back 40 1/2″ x 51″. Cut the umbrella's first and third sections. Cut the middle section of the clown's hat. Also cut the clown's left body and right arm. From the white, cut the front 28 1/2″ x 38 1/2″. From the pink with white dots, cut the clown's right body and left arm. Also cut the tip and handle of the umbrella and the pompom on the hat. From the orchid print, cut the second and fourth sections of the umbrella, the shoes, and the bottom ruffle on the hat. From the flesh, cut the hands and face. Cut the hair from the yellow. Cut the eyes from the purple, the nose and mouth from the hot pink, and the collar from the orchid and white stripe.

SEWING INSTRUCTIONS:

Cut the backing fabric the same size as the front and baste to the wrong side. Trace all the stitching lines onto the appliqués with the dressmaker's carbon paper. Using the photo as a guide, position the appliqués onto the quilt front and baste. Machine zigzag around the edges of the appliqués first, and then do the details as follows, using matching thread on all of the appliqués. Use a narrower stitch for the eyebrows in brown thread. Clip all the threads and remove the bastings from the appliqués.

Sew the border strips together and press seams. Sew on the brown pin stripe borders doing the sides first and then top and bottom. Remember to press after sewing on each border section. Sew the quilt front to the quilt back and batt by referring to the general instructions. Baste all three layers together. Machine quilt around the clown, umbrella, and on the inside edge of the brown pin stripe border. Remove bastings.

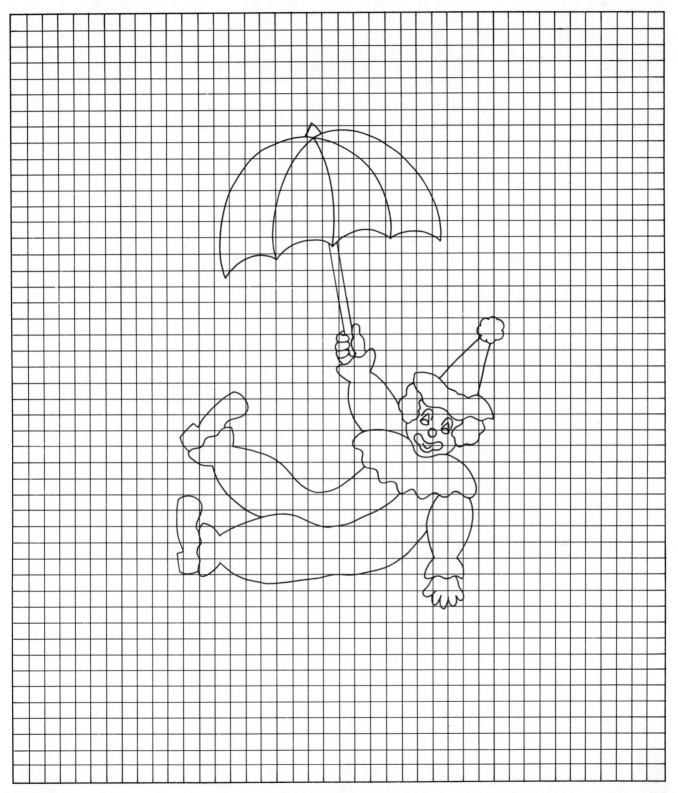

1 square = 1"

PINK FLAMINGOS

Mother and baby pink flamingos on a tropical island.

Finished size is 35 1/2" x 45 1/2"

FABRIC REQUIREMENTS:

2 yards tan
5/8 yard light green
3/4 yard light blue
1/4 yard hot pink
1/4 yard medium green
3/4 yard backing fabric
40 1/2" x 50 1/2" quilt batt
Thread: light green, medium green, light
    blue, tan, brown, and medium pink

CUTTING INSTRUCTIONS:

From the tan, cut border strips 4 1/2" wide by 4 5/8 yards long. Cut the back 40 1/2" x 50 1/2" and cut the palm tree trunk. From the light green, cut border strips 2" wide by 4 yards long and cut the mountain. From the light blue, cut the front 24 1/2" x 34 1/4". From the hot pink, cut the flamingos. From the medium green, cut the palm tree leaves and the grass section above the water.

SEWING INSTRUCTIONS:

Cut the backing fabric the same size as the front and baste to the wrong side. Trace all stitching lines onto the appliqués with dressmaker's carbon paper. Using the photo as a guide, position the appliqués onto the front and baste. Now trace the grass and water lines right onto the front. Machine zigzag around the edges of the appliqués first and then do the details as follows. Use the lighter pink thread on the flamingos and matching thread for the rest of the appliqué outlines. Stitch over the grass lines in light green thread and use light blue thread for the water lines. Use brown for the bark lines on the tree trunk. With black thread stitch the eyes by turning your stitch width control knob from narrow to wider and then back to narrow as you sew. Also stitch a narrow line of black along the lower section of beak. Clip all threads and remove all bastings from the appliqués.

Sew the border strips together and press seams. Sew on the light green borders doing the sides first and then the top and bottom. Remember to press seams after sewing on each border section. Do the same with the tan borders. Press the whole quilt front. Next, sew the quilt front to the quilt back and batt by referring to the general instructions. Baste all three layers together. Machine quilt across the top of the water, grass, and mountain, around the flamingos and palm tree. Also along both edges of the light green border. Remove bastings.

1 square = 1"

BALLOONS

These colorful balloons, a good choice for beginners, are so easy to appliqué.

Finished size is 35 1/2″ x 45″

FABRIC REQUIREMENTS:

2 yards pink
3/4 yard multi-colored plaid
3/4 yard white
1/8 yard blue
1/8 yard yellow
3/4 yard backing fabric
40 1/2″ x 50″ quilt batt
Thread: white, blue, yellow, and pink

CUTTING INSTRUCTIONS:

From the pink, cut individual strips which, when sewn together, will form one border 2″ wide by 4 3/4 yards long. Cut the back 40 1/2″ x 50″ and cut four balloons. From the plaid, cut twelve triangles. From the white, cut twelve triangles. From the blue, cut four balloons. From the yellow, cut four balloons.

SEWING INSTRUCTIONS:

From the backing fabric, cut twelve triangles and baste to the wrong sides of the white triangles. Sew a white triangle to a plaid triangle to form all the squares. Then, sew the squares together in rows of three. Now sew the four rows together to make the quilt front. Using the photo as a guide, position the balloons onto the white triangles and baste. Machine zigzag around the edges using matching thread. Clip all threads and remove the bastings from the appliqués.

Sew the border strips together and press seams. Sew on the pink borders sides first and then top and bottom. Be sure to press seams after sewing on each border section. Sew the quilt front to the quilt back and batt by referring to the general instructions. Baste all three layers together. Machine quilt around each balloon, along the diagonal seam of each square, and along the inside edge of the pink border. Remove bastings.

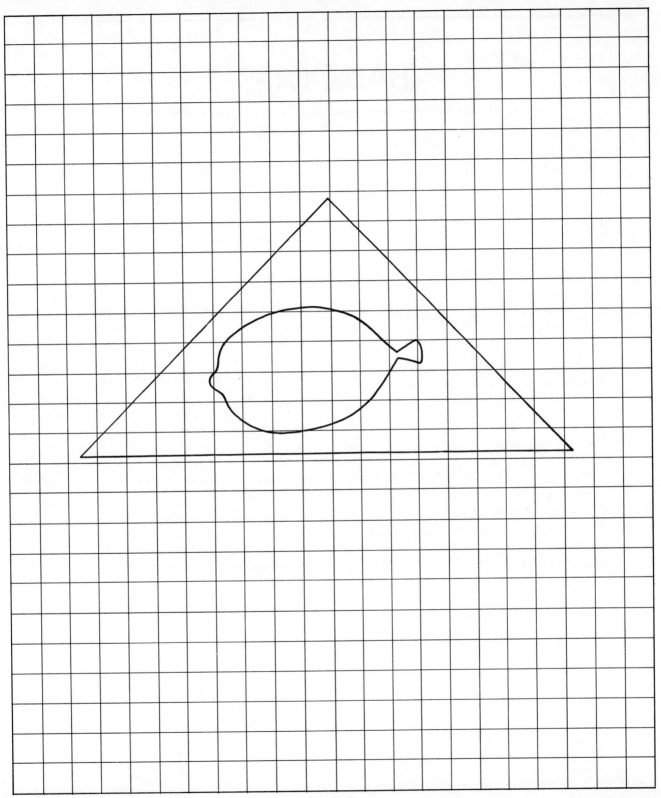

PICTURE FRAME

A little girl framed in polka-dots and trimmed with ribbon and lace.

Finished size is 34" x 43"

FABRIC REQUIREMENTS:

2 3/8 yards of rose and white polka dot
1/2 yard white
1/4 yard navy print
1/8 yard flesh
a scrap of navy
2 5/8 yards of 3/8" wide navy satin ribbon
1 1/2 yards of 1 1/8" wide white lace with
    ribbon center
1 yard backing fabric
39" x 48" quilt batt
Thread: navy, white, flesh, rose, and brown

CUTTING INSTRUCTIONS:

From the rose and white polka dot, cut the back 39" x 48" and the front 34 1/2" x 43 1/2". From the white, cut the large oval and the dress collar. From the navy print, cut the dress. From the flesh, cut the head, arms, and legs. From the scrap of navy, cut the shoes and the eyes.

SEWING INSTRUCTIONS:

Cut the backing fabric the same size as the front and baste to the wrong side. Trace all stitching lines onto the appliqués with the dressmaker's carbon paper. Using the photo as a guide, position the appliqués onto the quilt front and baste. Machine zigzag around the edges of the appliqués first and then do the details as follows. Use navy thread on the white oval and white thread for the details on the dress (not the edges). For the hair, nose, and eyebrows use a narrower stitch and brown thread. Use rose for the mouth. Use matching thread for the rest. Clip all threads and remove bastings from the appliqués.

With a straight stitch, sew on the lace diagonally across the upper left corner and the lower right corner so its center is 9 3/4" in from the corner edges. Now sew on the navy ribbon 1 1/8" from the edge of the lace on both sides. Press the whole quilt front. Sew the quilt front to the quilt back and batt by referring to the general instructions. Baste all three layers together. Machine quilt around the girl, white oval, and along each edge of the navy ribbon. Remove bastings.

1 square = 1″

BASKET OF PANSIES

Freshly picked purple pansies in a country basket.

Finished size is 36" x 43"

FABRIC REQUIREMENTS:

2 5/8 yards purple floral stripe
1/2 yard purple
1/2 yard beige
1/8 yard dark green
a scrap of light yellow and lavender
3/4 yard backing fabric
39" x 48" quilt batt
Thread: purple, dark green, dark brown,
    and light yellow

CUTTING INSTRUCTIONS:

From the purple floral stripe, cut border strips 4" wide by 4 3/8 yards long. Cut the back 39" x 48" and cut the front 26 1/2" x 32 1/2". From the purple, lavender, and light yellow, cut out the pansies by referring to the photo for a color guide. Also from the purple cut border strips 1 3/4" wide by 3 7/8 yards long. From the beige, cut the basket. From the dark green, cut the leaves.

SEWING INSTRUCTIONS:

Cut the backing fabric the same size as the front and baste to the wrong side. Trace all stitching lines onto the appliqués with dressmaker's carbon paper. Using the photo as a guide, position appliqués onto the quilt front and baste. Machine zigzag around the edges of the appliqués first and then do the details as follows. Use purple thread on all the sections of pansies except the oval in the center, which should be stitched in yellow. Use a narrower stitch and dark brown thread for the details of the basket. Use matching thread for the leaves. Clip all threads and remove the bastings from the appliqués.

Sew the border strips together and press seams. Sew on the purple borders doing the sides first and then the top and bottom. Remember to press seams after sewing on each border section. Now sew on the purple floral stripe borders in the same order. Sew the quilt front to the quilt back and batt by referring to the general instructions. Baste all three layers together. Machine quilt around the basket, pansies, and on both edges of the purple border. Remove bastings.

1 square = 1"

TOY SOLDIER

A toy soldier marching under the Christmas tree.

Finished size is 37'' x 43 1/2''

FABRIC REQUIREMENTS:

2 1/8 yards red
3/8 yard medium green corduroy
1/4 yard dark green
1/8 yard dark blue
1/8 yard yellow
3/8 yard white
3/4 yard red, green, and white print
a scrap of flesh, brown, and black
3/4 yard backing fabric
42'' x 48 1/2'' quilt batt
Thread: white, dark blue, red, yellow,
   green, brown, flesh, and black

CUTTING INSTRUCTIONS:

From the red, cut border strips 5'' wide by 4 1/2 yards long. Cut the back 42'' x 48 1/2''. Also cut the soldier's jacket, four round and two oblong ornaments, and the stripe on the soldier's hat. From the green corduroy, cut the tree. From the dark green, cut the floor. From the dark blue, cut the soldier's hat, pants, three round, and three oblong ornaments. From the yellow, cut the soldier's shoulder pads, the tree's stand, and star, also four round and one oblong ornament. From the white, cut border strips 2 1/4'' wide by 3 3/4 yards long, and the mopboard and trim on the soldier's jacket. From the red, green, and white print, cut the front 24 1/4'' x 31 1/2''. Cut the soldier's face and hands from the flesh. Cut the soldier's hair from the brown, and boots from the black.

SEWING INSTRUCTIONS:

Cut the backing fabric the same size as the front and baste to the wrong side. Trace all the stitching lines onto the appliqués with the dressmaker's carbon paper. Using the photo as a guide, position the appliqués onto the quilt front and baste. Machine zigzag around the edges first and then do the details as follows. Use white thread on all the sections of the soldier except the face, hair, hands, shoulder pads, and boots (use matching thread for these). Stitch in the eye with brown. Draw a line for the hat strap and stitch this in with dark blue thread. Stitch the tree outline, ornaments, star, and stand with matching thread. Stitch in the tree garland with white thread. Clip all threads and remove the bastings from the appliqués.

Sew the border strips together and press seams. Sew on the white borders doing the sides first and then top and bottom. Remember to press seams after sewing on each border section. Now sew on the red borders in the same order. Press the whole quilt front. Sew the quilt front to the quilt back and batt by referring to the general instructions. Baste all three layers together. Machine quilt around the soldier, tree, along the bottom edge of the mopboard, and on both edges of the white border. Remove bastings.

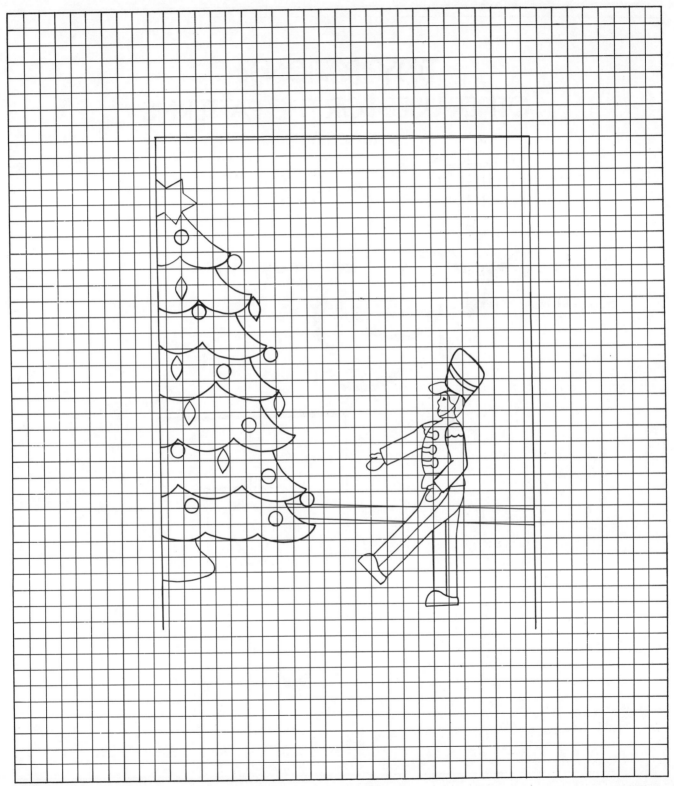

1 square = 1"

INSPIRATIONS:
OTHER USES FOR THE PATTERNS

MOBILES

WALL HANGING

BIB

BABY SACK

DRESSER DECORATION

FLOOR STENCILING

BED DECORATIONS

FOLDING SCREEN

WALL HANGING

APPLIQUÉ ON CHILDREN'S CLOTHES

TOTE BAG

It's a girl!

Sara Elizabeth
Feb. 6,   9 lbs. 6 oz.

BIRTH ANNOUNCEMENT

WINDOW SHADE

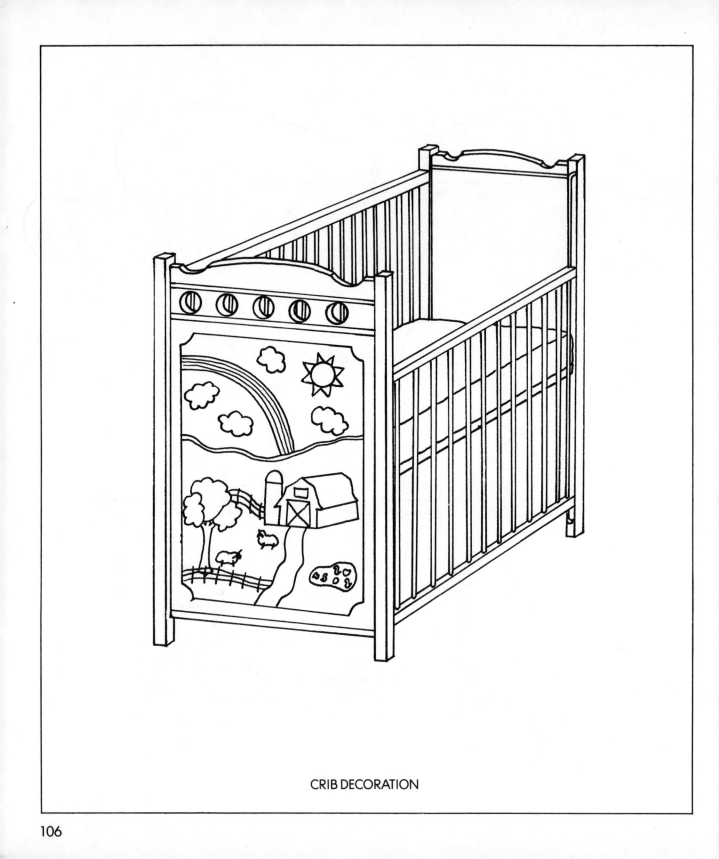

CRIB DECORATION

PILLOWS

TOY CHEST

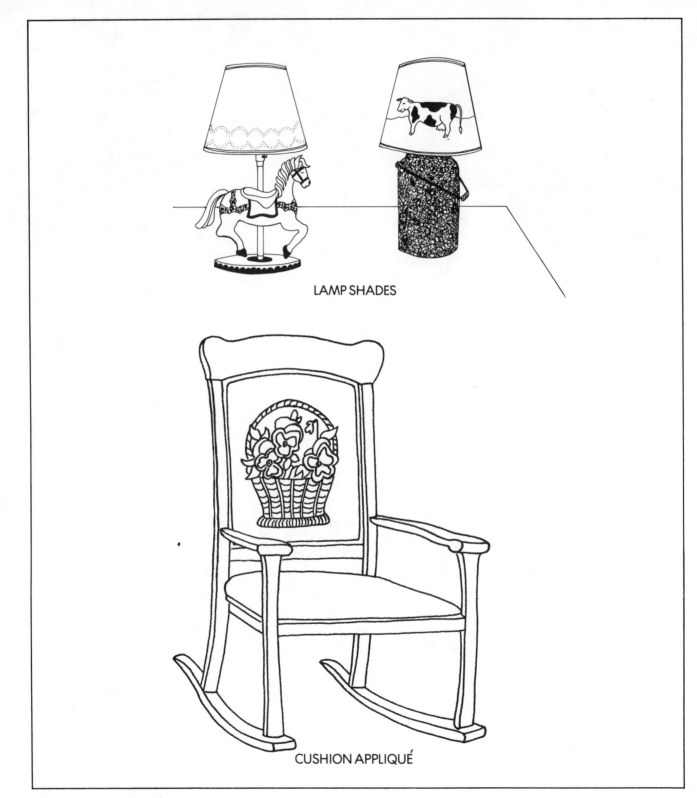

LAMP SHADES

CUSHION APPLIQUÉ

BATH AND TOWEL DECORATIONS

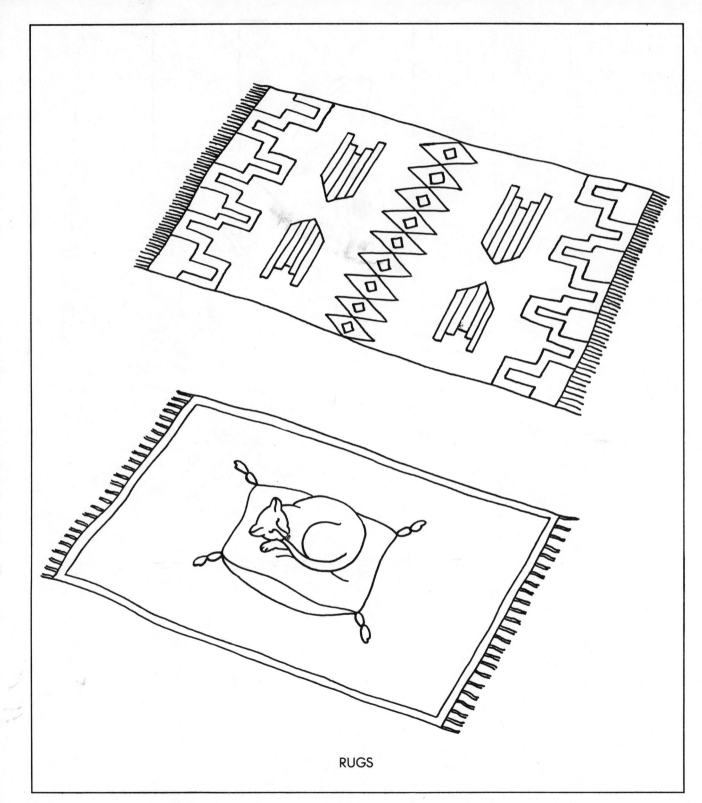

RUGS

PEG RACK

ACKNOWLEDGMENTS

A special thanks to my editor Adele Ursone for believing in this project from the very start, without whom this book would not have been possible.

My thanks and appreciation go to everyone who contributed to the making of this book. They are: Nancy Conrad, Judith Durell, Susan Harrington, Robert Hoebermann, Robert Jamback and Susan Morse Jamback, Linda Johnson, Larry McDonald, and Laurie Williams.

I want to thank my family for tolerating the disorderly conditions at home while I worked on this book. I quickly outgrew the sewing room, and there were fabric, paper, quilts, and patterns scattered around literally every room of the house.

And thank you, mother, for your encouragement and support.